PROPHETS
PITFALLS
AND
PRINCIPLES

GOD'S PROPHETIC PEOPLE
TODAY

by
DR. BILL HAMON

foreword by
Oral Roberts

CHRISTIAN INTERNATIONAL
P.O. Box 9000
Santa Rosa Beach, FL 32459
(904) 231-5308

edited by Paul Thigpen

| First Printing: | 20,000 | Third Printing: | 10,000 |
| Second Printing: | 20,000 | Fourth Printing: | 10,000 |

PROPHETS PITFALLS AND PRINCIPLES
God's Prophetic People Today

Library of Congress: 91-76413

International Standard Book Number:0-939868-05-9 (Vol. 3)
International Standard Book Number:0-939868-04-0 (Vol. 2)
International Standard Book Number:0-939868-03-2 (Vol. 1)
International Standard Book Number:0-939868-02-4 (Set)

produced by
CHRISTIAN INTERNATIONAL MINISTRIES

published by
DESTINY IMAGE
167 Walnut Bottom Road
Shippensburg, PA 17257-0310

FOREWORD
by
Oral Roberts

Bill Hamon, A Prophet For Our Time

I always take notice when Bill Hamon prophesies or writes a book on prophetic truths, or even if I'm just with him in prayer and discussion.

Bill's life in Jesus and Jesus' working His prophetic spirit through him, shows to the world—and the Body of Christ—that it's time we realized God has set in the Church not only pastors, evangelists and teachers but apostles and prophets (Eph.4:11).

I've known for a long time any of us who are "set in the Church" as a pastor, evangelist, teacher, prophet or apostle, operate under the apostolic and prophetic spirit of the Holy Spirit. Also at any time, anyone in one or more of these offices of the ministry, can manifest the spirit of apostle or prophet. In other words, the apostolic and prophetic covering is over all five offices. However, I also know there is a distinct office of each of these five, including that of the prophet.

To see Bill Hamon operating in the prophetic office, to see his humble spirit of giving God all the glory and his carefulness to line up all he says and does with the Word of God, is a blessing that I need, and, I believe, all the people of God need.

God bless Bill's new book *Prophets Pitfalls and Principles* to all who are blessed to read and study it. I thank God we are living in the days when God is placing a fresh, new emphasis on all the five offices of His Body, including that of the apostle and prophet.

DEDICATION

This book, "Prophets-3", is dedicated to all the leadership within the corporate Body of Christ. If the truths found within this book keep even one minister or Christian leader from falling prey to Satanic pitfalls and human character flaws, then it will be worth all that I have gone through to learn these lessons, including the endless hours it has taken to write this book. "Prophets-3" is dedicated to helping all God's people to be preserved blameless in body, soul and spirit unto the coming of the Lord.

APPRECIATION

Appreciation is given to my CI-NPM Board of Governors who, by their dedicated ministry and support, made it possible for their Bishop to take the time from his active traveling ministry to fulfill his commission from Christ to stay home and finish this desperately needed book. Heartfelt appreciation is given to my wife, Evelyn, for her encouragement for me to finish the book, and to the CI staff and CI-NPM ministers for carrying on the ministry while their President was writing.

CONTENTS

The Prophetic Movement vs. New Age Movement
Five Characteristics of Five-fold Ministry
Prophets Prophesying—Greatest Sign of Our Century

1. Are Old Testament Standards for Determining False Prophets Valid for New Testament Prophets and Prophetic Ministry?

2. What About Prophecies that Seem to Contradict One Another?

3. Does Prophecy Come to Pass According to Expectations?

4. Why Does God Allow False Prophets and Prophecies?

5. How Can We Weigh and Prove a Word to Be True Yet Have Faith in the Word of the Lord and Believe His Prophets?

6. Will the Person Receiving a True Prophetic Word Always Have a Witness That It Is Accurate and from God?

7. Is Prophetic Ministry Always the Pure Word of the Lord, or Contain Human Opinions, Applications or Interpretations?

8. Are Prophets Divinely Gifted by God to Minister Prophetically to Anyone Who Comes Before Them for Such Ministry?

9. Is It Possible to Prophesy a Person's Desire Even if the Desire Is in Conflict with God's Will for That Person's Life?

10. What Wrong Motives Must Prophets Avoid in Ministry?

11. What Are Proper Guidelines for Ministering Prophetic Words That Deal with Romance and Marriage?

12. What Are Proper Guidelines for Ministering Prophecies to the Sick or Dying Concerning Their Healing?

CAPITALIZATION

Dr. Hamon has taken *Author's Prerogative* in capitalizing certain words which are not usually capitalized according to the standard grammatical practice. This is done for the purpose of clarity and emphasis. Reference to the Church/Bride are capitalized because of Her union with Deity through Jesus Christ. **Prophets** are put in bold in a few places for emphasis. Company of Prophets is capitalized to designate a specific group of prophets. Prophetic Movement is capitalized as are all references to the major restorational movements within the Church. The word Scripture is capitalized only when referring to the whole Bible. Church and Body when referring to the universal Body of Christ the Church; church when referring to a denominational or local church. Logos/Word when referring to the whole Bible; rhema/word when referring to individual scriptures or prophetic words.

All scriptures are taken from King James versions (KJV, NKJV) except when designated. When quoting scripture the author sometimes adds **bold** or *italic* for emphasis.

1

GOD'S PREPARATION PROCESS
FOR
PITFALLS AND PRINCIPLES

I completed my Bible college training back in the 1950's with great ideas of changing the world for Jesus Christ. I was bold, fiery and ambitious. A statement I made over a national radio program at the time reveals how the president of the Bible College had inflamed my vision and faith: "People," I said, "I want you to know that this world is just so big. The devil is here and I am here, and one of us has got to go. I want you to know it's not going to be me."

The Lord took me from this world vision in Bible college to a small church in Yakima Valley, Washington. That church had enjoyed continuous revival every night for three years, but then the pastor had died, and the church had suffered split after split over just about every controversial doctrine that ever manifested itself among Pentecostals: doctrines of the Trinity, baptismal formulas, dress codes, church structure, and teachings of the Latter Rain movement.

When I arrived in February, 1954, there were just a handful of survivors who were hanging on, determinedly singing "I Shall Not Be, I Shall Not Be Moved". They had seen it all, done it all and been through it all, and they were determined that they would not be moved by anyone anymore.

God in His wisdom (and with a sense of humor, I think) set this young pip-squeak prophet in that place to pastor for the following six years. My faith and vision were sorely tried, sizzled and fried on the fires of God's process for making the man before manifesting the ministry.

During this time I watched great evangelists such as T.L Osborne, Oral Roberts and Billy Graham begin to affect the world with the powerful gospel of Jesus Christ. I would receive their magazines with their glowing reports. Instead of encouraging me, those reports would cause me great frustration and hours of agonizing before God as I tried to convince Him that He should have me out there doing the same thing and not stuck in that visionless local church.

As the old saying goes, I "died a thousand deaths" on the altar while complaining to God and trying to convince Him how desperately the dying souls around the world needed my mighty ministry more than this little remnant in the local church. But during those six years God worked on my maturity, manhood, motive and marriage. He took me from being a single man, nineteen years old and traveling as a prophetic evangelist, to being a married man with two sons, Tim and Tom. (Our daughter, Sherilyn, was born in 1961.)

While I was hid away at what I felt was a "back side of the desert with Moses" experience, I did not watch only the successful ministers. I also saw the decline and fall of many mighty deliverance evangelists in the late 1950's and early 1960's. Many of them I had admired and envied. But they began to fall because of the problems in the areas of morality, method, motive, message and money, with a lack of proper ministerial ethics.

From the depth of my spirit and from the personal prophecies that came over me from the prophetic presbytery, I knew that someday, someway, somehow my life and ministry were to affect the Church and world as a whole. I knew my destiny lay beyond the bounds of a local church. But as these great evangelists and a few prophets began to fall, the tragedy caused a great reverential fear of God to arise in my heart.

So I began to pray and seek God by the hour. One concern I prayed continually was phrased like this: "Lord I know that someday I will have a worldwide ministry similar to these men. What will keep me from falling as these men have fallen?"

My cry was to know the root problems that cause great ministers to fall and to have the wisdom to recognize the common deceitful and destructive pitfalls and character flaws. I desired to discern my own heart to recognize any tares of "weed seed" attitudes that could sprout, grow and eventually choke out my spiritual life and ministry. I earnestly prayed for God to do whatever necessary to purge and purify me before I ever reached the place where my life could and would affect tens of thousands.

I prayed for God to deal with me in my desert time of obscurity so that the minimum amount of people would be affected by my failures. During those many hours of prayer and personal Bible study, the Holy Spirit began to illuminate many scriptures to my mind that gave me some principles to practice and pitfalls to avoid. In those days of the mid 1950's these truths were in seed form, but now after almost forty years of ministry they have grown within my life and ministry to a harvestable crop.

These ripened grains of truth will be presented in this book. My prayer is that these truths concerning "principles to practice and pitfalls to avoid" will save many from falling while helping others to "be preserved blameless body, soul and spirit unto the coming of our Lord Jesus Christ" (1Thess.5:23). I pray these truths fall upon good ground that can produce thirty-, sixty- and a hundredfold.

May all of us have ears to hear what the Spirit has to say to each of us about biblical principles to practice and satanic pitfalls to avoid—so that we might take our place among God's great company of prophets, prophetic ministers and prophetic people.

FOUNDATIONS FOR PROPHETIC MINISTRY

Today God is bringing prophetic ministry to the attention of His people so that prophets and prophecy may be restored to their rightful place in the life of the Church. The prophetic movement is gaining momentum—and stirring controversy—as thousands of Christians seek answers to their questions about how God speaks to us through prophetic ministry, and how we should respond to His prophetic word.

For nearly forty years I have been deeply involved in such ministry, prophesying to tens of thousands and training others to prophesy as well. Several years ago God instructed me to begin writing several books that would help to clarify some of the most pressing issues in this area, both for prophetic ministers and for those receiving prophetic ministry. This is the third volume in the resulting series.

The first volume, *Prophets and Personal Prophecy*, answers the most common questions asked by those who have received a personal prophetic word from God. It includes guidelines for receiving and responding properly to such prophecies. It also provides numerous examples from Scripture and my personal ministry experience that illustrate how God may speak about various areas of our life, such as divine healing; ministries, gifts, and callings; romance and marriage; business endeavors; pregnancies and births; and major decisions and geographical moves.

The second volume, *Prophets and the Prophetic Movement*, focuses on the restorational move of God that is presently taking place to restore prophets and prophecy to the Church. It was written to establish the reality and describe the extent of the Prophetic Movement. By providing biblical and historical information, it also helps those who participate in that movement to understand its history; to derive all the benefits from the truths and spiritual experiences that are a part of the movement; and to receive guidelines and wisdom that they may maintain what they have received with integrity and balance while not losing the power or purpose of God for this restorational move of the Holy Spirit.

This third volume, *Prophets Pitfalls and Principles*, seeks to answer questions and provide help for the prophetic minister. It presents proper principles for ministering personal prophecy, warns of the major pitfalls of prophetic ministry, and above all focuses on the qualities of personal character necessary for mature ministry.

The insights of the first two volumes provide a critical foundation for ministering prophetically.

2

PITFALLS FOR PROPHETIC MINISTERS

God's Sovereign Choice. The Scriptures clearly teach that saints do not choose their membership ministry within the Body of Christ: "God hath set the members in the Body as it pleased him" (1Cor.12:18). Nor do ministers call themselves to a five-fold ministry of their own choosing. Remember that Jesus said to His twelve ministers: "You have not chosen me, but I have chosen you and ordained you" (John 15:16). Paul went on to say: "When Christ ascended on high he gave gifts unto men. **He** gave some to be apostles, some prophets, some evangelists, some pastors and teachers" (Eph.4:8,11). And Paul insisted that it is "God [who] hath set in the Church apostles and prophets" (1Cor.12:28).

The gifts and callings of God are based on His sovereignty, not on human worthiness or persistence in requesting a position. The principle Paul revealed when he said, "Behold the **goodness** and the **severity** of God," (Rom.11:22) applies to God's choice for ministry. The goodness of God is manifested in His gifts and callings. His severity is revealed in the process of His training to make a person ready to be commissioned to that calling.

To Whom Much is Given, Much Is Required. Jesus has a special love for and dedication to those whom He has called to represent Him. The Lord has a precious investment in them: He has given them of His own nature, grace, gifts and ministry, and

7

to whom much is given, much is required (Lk.12:48). Those who are called to this realm of ministry will be judged more strictly than others (James 3:1).

This principle seems to apply especially to those called to be prophets. Those whom He calls to speak directly for Him with a "Thus saith the Lord" are given much. But in the same way much more is required of them in obedience, integrity, righteousness and Christlikeness in all areas of life.

The devil hates God's prophets. So he has developed a whole arsenal of weapons of destruction to use against them. He has dug a pit for every prophetic minister and is determined to cause each one to fall in that pit and be buried. I call these snares of Satan "prophetic pitfalls."

In the first volume of this series on prophets and the prophetic ministry we dealt primarily with guidelines for those who receive a prophetic word and desire to respond to it properly. In this volume we are addressing those who speak the prophetic word, offering guidelines for ministering with integrity and accuracy, and warnings about the pitfalls the devil has prepared for them. This section will deal in particular with many of the snares that can hinder prophets and their prophetic message. We will derive most of the principles to practice and pitfalls to avoid from the examples of biblical characters, primarily prophets and apostles.

My personal burden is more than just activating into ministry those called to be prophets. I also want to teach and train them in such a way that they will maintain their prophetic ministry in power and purity until they reach their predestined purpose: to be conformed to the image of Jesus Christ, the Prophet (Rom.8:29). Christ was the fullness of all the five-fold ministries in one human body (Col.2:9). He is the perfect pattern for all New Testament ministers, including the prophet.

WEED SEED ATTITUDES AND ROOT PROBLEMS

I was raised on a farm in Oklahoma and learned there much about the farmer's problems with weed seeds and grass roots. In my high school agriculture classes we had to study all kinds of seeds. We learned that some weed seeds and some good crop seeds look so much alike that the difference is difficult to determine while they are still in seed form. Only extensive education and experience allows a farmer to recognize a seed immediately for what it truly is.

The same is true with the attitudes of our hearts. To recognize and identify a "weed seed" attitude within a person—that is, an attitude that will eventually sprout into a dangerous weed of wrong behavior—requires someone with understanding and experience in spiritual discernment.

An Illustration from the Natural Realm. One plant that most clearly typifies in the natural realm the development of root problems in the spiritual realm is the weed called Johnson grass. This variety of grass has joints every one to six inches along each branch of its root system. These roots are myriad, running in every direction and intertwining themselves with the root system of a good crop, such as corn.

When Johnson grass sprouts and begins to grow alongside a sprout of corn, the two plants look almost identical. If the Johnson grass is allowed to grow alongside that stalk of corn until both are about knee high, their root systems become so intertwined that the Johnson grass cannot be pulled up by the roots without also uprooting and destroying the corn. The best the farmer can do to preserve the corn is to cut the grass off at ground level.

The problem, however, is that the Johnson grass will immediately send up new shoots, both from the stub of the old shoots and from the underground joints in the roots. You cannot destroy the roots simply by cutting off the plants. You can only keep it from growing to full maturity and producing a head of seeds.

Meanwhile, the root system of the grass continues to steal nutrients from the soil that should go to the cornstalk. So at most the cornstalk may be able to produce a scrawny, inferior ear of corn unqualified to be used as seed corn for the next planting.

God's Severe Remedy. We should note that because of the severity of the problem, the farmer cannot remedy it permanently during the growing season. Since Johnson grass has blades like corn, the farmer cannot spray the grass without killing the corn. All that can be done is to wait until that season is over and then plow up the soil to expose the roots. Then the roots can be raked and burned or poisoned, or else left to be killed by a hard freeze in the winter. Only after the harvest season, during the winter, can farmers deal with grass root problems (just as they must wait till winter to prune fruit trees).

In the spiritual realm as well, God will not deal with advanced root problems during a productive ministry season. He will bring the minister and his or her ministry into a winter season of inactivity and non-productivity. He will plow the prophet upside-down, exposing the root problems, and then He will either spray them with a strong anointing to destroy them or else rake the minister's soul until all the roots are removed and thrown into the fire of God's purging purpose.

For that reason, we must allow God and those He has appointed as our spiritual overseers to show us our weed seed attitudes and remove the newly-sprouted character flaws before they grow intertwined with our personality and performance. The longer we wait, the more drastic the process becomes.

These Truths for All People Everywhere: Although this book is addressed primarily to prophets and prophetic ministers, these truths are vital to every five-fold minister, Christian leader, or ministering member of the Body of Christ. The **principles to practice and pitfalls to avoid apply to every Christian.** So I encourage you as you read the following pages to allow the Holy Spirit to illuminate your mind and soul to any character flaws, weed seed attitudes, root problems, or "prophet syndromes" you may have.

If you have had a particular problem for awhile and it has been manifested more than three times, I believe it has gone beyond the seed stage and has now sprouted. So it must be dealt with immediately before its root system becomes intertwined with your personality and performance.

Today God is purging individuals, as well as His Church as a whole, of all the things that are contrary to His own nature and character. If we allow God to purge us, we will be made a vessel of honor. If not, God will remove us from ministry in His Body, just as sheep are separated from goats, good fish from bad fish, and tares from wheat (Mt.25:32,33; 13:29,30,47,48).

3

PROPHET ELIJAH PITFALL

You probably know the story of Elijah and the prophets of Baal. But take a few minutes just now to reread the account in 1 Kings chapters 17 through 19 to refresh your knowledge of the principal characters and events involved.

Elijah demonstrated many qualities that are admirable in a prophet of God: prayer, faith, obedience to the voice of the Lord, and a willingness to put his life on the line to prove that Jehovah was the true God. He stood alone as the prophet of God and challenged eight hundred and fifty prophets of Baal to a contest on Mount Carmel that would demonstrate whose God was sovereign. That day he also challenged the people of Israel to choose whom they would serve—God or Baal—based on the outcome of the contest.

In the ensuing events, the prophets of Baal showed themselves and their god to be impotent. But Elijah prayed a short prayer, and God sent fire from heaven to consume the sacrifice. Elijah thus exposed the false prophets and proved Jehovah to be the true God. Then he killed all the prophets of Baal, interceded to break the three-year drought he had prophesied for the land, and outran all of Ahab's chariot horses. In light of these events, we might reasonably assume that such a fierce, effective and powerful prophet would be without character flaws and immune to satanic pitfalls.

A Pit of Self-Pity. Nevertheless, the rest of the story shows otherwise. When Queen Jezebel heard that Elijah had killed all

13

of her prophets, she decreed the same fate for him. This reaction from the leadership of the land caused him to plunge from the peak of powerful prophetic performance into the pit of self-pity and pessimistic prayer.

Elijah ran clear out of the land of Israel and fled to the wilderness. He sat down under a juniper tree and prayed that God would kill him. Of course, such self-pitying prayers were hypocritical in those circumstances, because if Elijah had really wanted to die, he needed only to stay where Jezebel was, and she would have gladly answered his death-wish prayer.

Elijah portrays the prophet who is mighty in prophesying and in powerful performance, but weak in personality, attitude, and adjustments to rejection and persecution. We should note that God did not answer his prayers for death in the way he had hoped, but rather by turning up the fire of purification until all the dross of his self-life could be burned out.

The prophetic ministry often places the prophet in extreme situations with high stakes: success or failure, acceptance or rejection, vindication or humiliation, life or death. When great success results, victories are won and great revival takes place, the prophet usually expects church leadership to appreciate his or her prophetic words and powerful performances. Yet often such leadership reacts instead as Queen Jezebel did—not only with rejection, but with threats of destruction. Consequently, the prophet may grow deeply discouraged.

Descending by Steps. Prophets reach the bottom of this pit of despair by descending steps, beginning with disappointment. If the situation is not immediately adjusted with a proper attitude, such disappointment will lead next to discouragement, then resentment, self-pity, a persecution complex, and anger. The final step for prophets who climb down into this pit is a bitter and hard critical spirit that causes them to be a law unto themselves, with such a spirit of rejection that no one can reach them in their self-delusion.

disappointment → discouragements →
resentment →

This prophetic pitfall causes the man or woman of God to develop a weed seed attitude of self-pity like Elijah, saying: "Everybody is against me. Nobody understands my ministry. I'm alone under the juniper tree. Nobody appreciates my great accomplishment of turning Israel from idols to the true God. I even ended their famine by bringing rain; I destroyed all the oppressive false prophets. But they don't appreciate anything I've done."

Such thinking sends prophets into what I call the "cave mentality." In that condition, they come to believe as Elijah did: "I'm the only one left!"

Sadly enough, ministers who make this mistake of thinking that they are the only ones left in the ministry with a true message, anointed ministry and proper vision will open themselves up to the spirit of error. Their doctrine may remain true, but their spirit becomes wrong. If that spirit is not adjusted quickly, they may become subject to an array of spiritual problems.

They may develop an exclusive, seclusive spirit that forms a cult group. They may become an instrument of Satan to sow discord or suspicion in the Body of Christ. They may fall into personal immorality. Or they may backslide completely and become a reprobate castaway.

A Spirit of Error. In forty years of ministry I have seen this process occur many times. For example, in the Faith movement I once heard of a minister who had written several books and thus became a recognized teacher in some circles. A few years later he put out a tape saying that he was the only one who still preached the pure faith message. He developed the prophet syndrome that whines, "I alone am left."

When I heard that tape, I told the person who had asked me to listen to it that the brother speaking on it had developed a spirit of error. I added that if he were not checked, he would take a truth and turn it into a cult. Sadly enough, it wasn't long before scores of Christians died because of his erroneous spirit and extreme emphasis on a particular truth. The leader himself died an early death because he had come into bondage to his own spirit and teaching.

On another occasion, in the late 1980's, I heard a leading television evangelist say publicly on his broadcast that he was the only one God had left to evangelize the world. Within a few months the scandal of his immoral behavior was the talk of both the Church and the secular media. Pride caused his downfall, but his root problem was the Elijah syndrome with its resulting cave mentality.

To avoid a similar outcome in our own lives, we prophetic ministers need to grow to the place of wisdom and maturity that will allow us to weather such occasions without losing hope. Those of us who develop the Elijah weed seed attitude must remember what God spoke to that prophet when he said, "I alone am left." The Lord let him know that seven thousand others were just as righteous and dedicated as he, with a similar vision for God's cause.

Wake Up and Shake Loose. I myself have been in this pit a few times in my life, and I've met a number of others who felt they were the only ones in their church or nation who had God's true heart and vision. If you have succumbed to the "I alone am left" syndrome, then know for sure that God has thousands of other prophetic ministers dedicated to His burden and vision. Let the truth set you free to act upon the words of the prophet Isaiah's admonition: "Shake thyself from the dust… arise…loose thyself from the bands about thy neck" (Is.52:2).

In plain words, this means get out of your self-pity party, your martyrdom-persecution complex. Shake loose from that exclusive, seclusive spirit, that inflated sense of self-importance. Wake up and put on the strength of Christ's nature, adjusting your wrong attitude before it develops a root system that will sap the life of Christ from you.

Respond as quickly as you would if a rattlesnake had fallen on your head. And if the truth has not dawned on you sufficiently to set you free, then find help fast from a senior minister before you backslide, fall into the spirit of error, or sink so deeply into self-delusion that you self-destruct.

My fellow prophetic minister, if you have given in to the "cave mentality," then remember that God only had two things to say to the prophet while he was in the cave. The first was a question he asked and repeated: "What are you doing here, Elijah?" The second was this: "Get out of the cave and get on the mountain before the Lord to listen for the voice of God."

Elijah obeyed that command, and when he did, God gave him a great commission to carry His purposes on for many years, even after Elijah was taken to heaven. If we want our ministries to continue in fruitfulness, we too must come out of the self-pity of the cave mentality to hear the voice of God more clearly (1Kings 19:13-17).

Continual Criticism Is a Warning Sign. I have found that any minister—whether apostle, prophet, pastor, teacher, or evangelist—who begins to criticize other ministers and imply that he or she is the role model for all ministry has some serious root problems, weed seed attitudes, and hidden sins. Ministers who devote the majority of their preaching and prophesying to criticizing other Christian ministries become motivated by the spirit of deception, prideful self-delusion, and the same kind of self-importance demonstrated by Lucifer himself. This behavior is one of the most deadly sins of the ministry, especially the prophetic ministry.

The line between pronouncing God's genuine prophetic judgments and ministering out of a wounded heart or spirit of rejection is a thin one. That is why all prophets need to be related and accountable to someone they trust enough to allow that person to be the spiritual surgeon who operates on their

spirit and attitude. The spiritually diseased area must be surgically removed, the wound must be cleansed and closed properly, and time must be given for healing and restoration in those
areas of the person's life.

A Recent Example. Some time ago, one of the prophets in the
Christian International Network of Prophetic Ministries began
manifesting the Elijah syndrome attitudes we have described.
So the Bishop and the Board of Governors had to discipline the
person involved.

This prophet had an effective and anointed prophetic ministry. His prophecies were accurate and powerful. Healings and
other miracles were manifested in his ministry.

Nevertheless, not all of his "10 M's" were in order. His message, ministry and morality were all right, but his maturity, motive, methods, and ministerial ethics were far enough out of line
to require immediate attention. The "Johnson grass" root
problems that had sprouted in his life were growing just as
rapidly as his ministry.

The Bishop and the Board of Governors came to the conclusion that this prophet had a spiritually contagious disease
that needed to be "surgically" removed. In fact, we told him he
had a "blind spot" in his life that prevented him from seeing the
gravity of his situation.

All thirty ministers present at the meeting agreed that the
root problem was serious enough to require the prophet to
withdraw from public ministry for a season. We offered to bring
him to our ministry's campus for an extended time of ministry
until he was delivered, healed, transformed and reinstated in
public ministry.

Sad to say, this prophet allowed us to cut the "Johnson
grass" of the problem during our meeting with him—but as it
turned out, he wouldn't let us walk with him through a "winter
season" withdrawn from public ministry so that God could
destroy the deep weed roots in his heart.

The prophet finally talked himself into believing that all the other thirty ministers were wrong, and he alone was right. His conclusion was a classic statement of self-deception: "You say I have a blind spot concerning my problems, but I don't see it." In the end, he resorted to the typical excuse of all those who are more "spiritual" than mature, and who want to do their own thing: "God told me," he said, "that I am not to submit to your discipline but to continue my great ministry to the Church." This minister had the potential to become a great pillar of truth and a father of the faith during his lifetime—if he had only submitted to the counsel of his Bishop and the board of elders.

What is the use of being related and submitted to a ministerial organization if we're not as willing to receive its disciplinary counsel and correction as we are to receive its blessing and help in promoting our ministry? We must remember that the Bible insists that those who are unwilling to submit to discipline and correction are not true children of God, and their ministry is illegitimate. "If you are not disciplined, then you are illegitimate children and not true sons" (Heb.12:8).

Receive Everything with Grace. There is no limit to how much God can use people who are able to receive support and correction, praise and persecution with the same gracious spirit. Such ministers can handle success without being lifted up in pride, and endure rejection and seeming failure without growing overly discouraged. God grant that we can learn to be praised for powerful prophetic performances without becoming proud, and to be criticized or disciplined without developing a persecution complex.

Prophets must develop Christ's character, which is able to receive both positive and negative responses with consistent grace. The only way the last-day prophets in the army of the Lord will be able to survive is to maintain a proper attitude and steadfast walk with the Lord Jesus, whether we are received or rejected by the people and the leadership of the Church.

pg 14 + 15 Elijah — mighty in prophesying + in power performance, but had a weed seed of self pity attitude.

Elijah syndrome — I alone am left.

4

PROPHETS JEREMIAH AND EZEKIEL'S PROBLEM WITH PERSECUTION

Ezekiel and Jeremiah probably suffered more severe personal persecution than any other biblical prophets. Their prophecies were rejected and the people rebelled against them more than most. God had to warn Ezekiel: "They are a rebellious house....And thou, son of man, be not afraid of them, neither be afraid of their words, though briers and thorns be with thee, and thou dost dwell among scorpions" (Eze.2:6). Jeremiah, for his part, was rewarded for his ministry by being thrown into the stocks, a prison, and a miry dungeon (Jer.20:2; 37:15; 38:6).

Suffering Is Standard for the Prophetic Life. The principal players in the biblical story—God, humanity and the devil—are still the principal players today, and though we live under a new covenant, these characters have not changed. God still speaks through His prophets, people still resent and resist God's prophetic word, and the devil still does all he can to destroy the prophets. So persecution and suffering are all part of the prophet's cross to bear.

Jesus said that unless we are willing to take up our cross and deny ourselves, we cannot be disciples (Mt.16:24). How much more does this principle apply to being prophets? Prophets must take up their ministry crosses joyfully, denying themselves all the fleshly indulgences of these prophetic pitfalls, weed seed attitudes and syndromes.

James wrote that we must take the prophets as an example of suffering affliction (James 5:10). He did not say to take the priests, Levites, kings, scribes, or pastors as an example of suffering, but rather the prophets. So I think Peter may have had the prophets and apostles especially in mind when he wrote: "Think it not strange concerning the fiery trials which come to test your quality of manhood as though something strange and unusual to you and your position were befalling you" (1Pet.4:12, AMP).

No—such circumstances are not **strange**, but rather **standard**, for prophets. Just as the gift of unknown tongues comes with the baptism of the Holy Spirit, so persecution comes with prophetic ministry. All five-fold ministers, and in fact "all that will live godly in Christ Jesus," will suffer persecution (2Tim.3:12). Yet my experience leads me to believe that the role of prophets naturally produces more persecution and suffering for them than the role of most other ministers. So all who feel called to be a prophet, to be a prophetic minister, or even simply to move in the spirit or gift of prophecy must adjust their attitude accordingly.

Grace to Adjust. We who are called to be prophets have no option except to adjust to the reality of this matter. If you cannot take rejection, persecution, and pressure from peers, then you cannot serve as one of God's end-time prophets. But God's enabling grace always comes along with His calling if we will appropriate it by faith and obedience. Prophets must endure suffering, persecution and rejection without developing a persecution complex or a spirit of rejection. This is the truth—truth that, according to Jesus, will set us free (John 8:32); truth that, according to Peter, is cause for rejoicing and giving thanks (1Pet.4:13).

Paul received the understanding from God that the more revelation we receive of God's secrets, the more thorns of persecution and demonic opposition we must endure (2Cor.12:7-10).

Since apostles as well as prophets have received the revelation ministry, (Eph.3:5) then we know what to expect when the apostles are fully restored to the Church and we have both prophets and apostles in full operation. There will come not only a double portion of anointing, but also a greater flow of opposition and persecution, especially from that part of the religious world that rejects present truth.

5

PROPHET ABRAHAM AND FAMILY PROBLEMS

People in the service professions, such as ministry, medicine, law, politics, and police work, seem to have the greatest stress in their personal family life. Prophet Abraham's greatest trials and problems came from his family. His root problem and pitfall was allowing family influences to hinder him from obeying God completely in order to fulfill God's personal word to him.

Family Pressures. To start with, Abraham's love for his family, pressure from his relatives, and a sense of obligation to his parents caused him to take his family with him when he left Ur of the Chaldees. This was only a partial obedience to his personal prophecy, and it hindered the fulfillment of his ministry for a period of time. He consequently settled down before he reached Canaan, living in Haran for several years. He stayed there until his father died, before he came into his Canaan ministry (Gen.11:31-12:4).

Again, it was a family member—nephew Lot, whom Abraham was to have left behind—that caused a split in Abraham's followers after considerable growth in his Canaan ministry (Gen.13:1-11). Abraham's prophet pitfall was to allow the wrong type of family influence in his decision making. The problem emerged once more when his wife Sarah influenced him to take Hagar, her Egyptian handmaiden, as a surrogate mother to produce the promised seed. The results of yielding to that advice cost him dearly as a father, producing an Ishmael ministry that has persecuted and opposed the prophesied Isaac ministry down to this day (Gen.16).

We Are Not to Be Dictators. We should note here, of course, that this does not imply that prophets are to be dictators in their homes. A married prophet or prophetess is to be a co-laborer with his or her mate, and the two of them ideally should move in unity and with a mutual witness. Even the children should be trained and involved in knowing the mind of Christ for the family and making prophetic decisions.

Nevertheless, there are times when God reveals His will clearly to the prophet, and as priest of his home he must take a firm stand in waiting patiently until God's way for his personal prophecy to be fulfilled is revealed. Family members sometimes have a way of putting pressure on the prophet to take the initiative to fulfill prophecy. Most often these family members are being motivated by their own convictions rather than divine directives about the when, where and how of fulfilling a word.

I can remember times like this in my own life when I had to stand firm on what I knew God had spoken to me, although some of my family members were not ready to do so. Even so, I want to emphasize that I typically make no major decisions nor take any major actions without the agreement of my wife, and usually of our adult children as well. I believe that when things are done in God's timing and way, a couple will experience mutual witness and agreement.

Every family situation is unique, so it is impossible to present firm rules in this matter that would be binding on every family. I can understand and feel compassion for the situation in which some prophets find themselves when their family is not as spiritual, committed, and properly related to God as they are. My wife and children share my priorities and commitments, so I cannot judge others with a different situation. We simply must recognize that some cases involve sensitive and complex issues that must be dealt with on an individual basis as a prophet seeks to obey divine directives and yet maintain godly family relationships.

Though the Bible tells us how Abraham allowed his family to influence him wrongly, it never records that God rebuked Abraham specifically for allowing relatives to hinder the fulfillment of his personal prophecies in that way. I believe this reveals God's own high priority for family structures and relationships. After all, He created the family before prophets and the Church even came into existence. So I believe a person must have a direct command from God, pastoral confirmation and several other confirmations from mature ministers before acting upon any personal prophetic word that would hinder family relationships.

The Spoiled Child Syndrome. When we read in the Bible about the Israelite priest Eli and his sons, we discover what I would call the "spoiled child syndrome." This problem is common among "PK's" (preacher's kids), but it can crop up in any family where the parents indulge their children inappropriately. The destructive results can last long beyond childhood and can undermine the son's or daughter's potential for ministry.

We're told that "Eli's sons were wicked men; they had no regard for the Lord" (1Sam.2:12 NIV). More specifically, they abused their position as ordained ministers of God by taking more than their rightful share of the people's offerings to God. According to Scripture, "this sin of the young men was very great in the Lord's sight, for they were treating the Lord's offering with contempt" (v.17).

What was Eli's response to the situation? Rather than disciplining his sons, he looked the other way. So God rebuked Eli through a prophet, asking, "Why do you honor your sons more than me...?" (v.29). When the father failed to correct his sons, he was putting them ahead of God. Judgment came upon their household when God decreed to Eli: "All your descendants will die in the prime of life" (v.33).

In light of the televangelist scandals a few years ago, we should keep in mind the severity of this situation and its potential for devastation in the Church. Today's spoiled children will be tomorrow's unethical ministers, taking more than their rightful share of the money from God's people in order to pamper themselves, and thus "treating the Lord's offering with contempt." We must not fall prey to this ministerial syndrome as we seek to honor God first by disciplining our children properly.

Mentors Model Methods. We should also note here that the prophet Samuel, who was mentored in ministry by old Eli, evidently repeated some of his child-rearing practices. When Samuel grew old, he appointed his own two sons as judges for Israel (1Sam.8:1). "But his sons did not walk in his ways," the Scriptures say. "They turned aside after dishonest gain and accepted bribes and perverted justice" (v.3).

The consequences of their sin went far beyond their immediate family. Not only did Samuel's sons prevent justice in the land. Their behavior also incited the people to demand a king and reject God's leadership of their nation (vv.4-7).

This series of biblical events illustrates that ministers typically take on the principles and practices of their mentors. Eli modeled the "spoiled child syndrome" for Samuel, just as King David was later to model sexual excess for his son Solomon. In contrast, God declared that one of the reasons for Him decreeing continual blessings to Abraham's descendants was "For I know him, that he will command his children and his household after him, and they shall keep the way of the LORD, to do justice and judgment; that the LORD may bring upon Abraham that which he has spoken of him" (Gen.18:19). God saw that Abraham would not spoil his child but would properly discipline and train him up in the way he should live and be (Prov.22:6).

The Deception of "Ministerial Mates". In my years as a bishop over many ministers, I have had to deal with a number of deceptions that lead ministers into destruction. Over the last thirty years one deception I have often heard is the concept of a "ministerial mate" or a "spiritual spouse." This notion has grown throughout the Christian ministry in general and has even crept into the Prophetic movement. In fact, it seems to have made greater inroads into those circles where there are claims of revelation knowledge and prophetic direction.

A "ministerial mate" or "spiritual spouse" is anyone a married minister (or any Christian person) allows to become a closer companion than his or her true spouse, especially when that person is of the opposite sex. It is usually an associate minister, secretary, or worship or youth leader. For a married person to cultivate romantic feelings or actions or sexual involvement with someone other than his or her marriage partner is sin in God's sight. So this kind of inappropriate closeness is dangerous because it usually leads to romance and finally to sexual immorality.

A Gradual Process of Bonding and Deception. Of course, this situation does not happen overnight. Typically, a minister and an associate or secretary work closely together over months and years until a "soul tie" develops—that is, a close emotional bonding. The minister's spouse ceases to be his or her closest friend, counselor, sounding board and co-laborer in the ministry. The minister begins to spend more time with the associate at the office and out of town at conferences than with the spouse at home.

As this deception takes root within the minister, he or she takes further actions to fulfill its ultimate purpose. The minister's spouse is manipulated out of active ministry with the minister and the church, with an accompanying alienation of affections within the marriage. The minister justifies such actions by claiming that the "ministerial mate" is more understanding and appreciative than the spouse. The "mate" seems patient, kind, sweet and trusting, while the spouse appears as fussy and demanding, always questioning why the minister has to be away from home so much and spends so little time with the family.

The Spouse Must Take Action. Sin and lust are deceitful, blinding a person to reality until the deception leads to its final result: an adulterous affair that destroys the minister's marriage, ministry and character. So a minister's spouse who senses such a situation developing needs to bring it to the attention of the minister. If the minister responds with understanding, begins immediately to adjust the situation, and works toward restoring a proper relationship with the family, then the spouse need mention it to no one else.

On the other hand, if the minister responds with resentment, accusing the spouse of jealousy, lack of commitment, or failure to understand ministerial responsibilities, then the spouse's obligation is to go immediately to their spiritual overseer, telling all and getting the overseer involved in the situation. The spouse must not be stopped by threats or a spirit of intimidation intended to keep them from getting help. The situation will not improve simply by being ignored or by the spouse's keeping silent in hopes that time will work it out. Prayer will help, but this particular situation is usually not resolved without proper outside help.

Remember: Revealing this problem to a spiritual overseer does not mean someone is betraying a confidence, failing to stand by his or her spouse, or failing to cover the sin with love. In this case, the scriptural command "Open rebuke is better than secret love" (Prov.27:5) supercedes the scriptural principle "Love covers a multitude of sins" (1Pet.4:8). The longer a spouse waits to get help, the more the situation will deteriorate, increasing the possibility that both the marriage and the ministry will be dissolved.

Avoid this prophetic pitfall and character flaw at all costs. When all things are in divine order, then the proper priorities and responsibilities are these: first God, then family, then ministry. All other areas should be taken care of only after these three areas of responsibility are fulfilled.

Abrahams pitfall he allowed.
family influences in his life.
ie Lot, Sara + others.

Eli - faul to discipline his
sons.

6

PROPHET MOSES AND OVERPROTECTIVENESS

Moses was a prophet who also had to fulfill the role of pastoring three million of God's people. He carried the pastoral rod and staff in his hand to shepherd and lead God's people from Egyptian bondage to freedom in the wilderness, and, according to prophecy, he was to have taken them into the promised land. But Moses had a human virtue that became a vice—a personal strength that, when taken to the extreme, became a double weakness.

A Danger for Prophetic Pastors. Moses' pitfall—one that kept him from fulfilling his personal prophecy about entering Canaan—came about through a dilemma faced by all prophetic pastors. He was torn between human mercy and compassion on the one hand, and God's judgment and prophetic purpose on the other. Moses' root problem was being overprotective of his personal pastoral flock and too insistent that God had to preserve the established generation instead of starting afresh.

When Moses stood between the wrath of God and the disobedience of the people (Ex.32:7-14), he provided a type of our Lord Jesus Christ, the intercessor and mediator between God and humanity. But this attitude of Moses has another side we must recognize. From the perspective of God's prophetic purposes, Moses' attitude was a hindrance to the fulfilling of his full ministry prophesied to him by the great I AM Himself.

During those wilderness days, the Israelites tempted God ten times with murmuring and complaining (see Num.14:22).

33

God repeatedly told Moses that his congregation was full of stiff-necked, self-willed saints who belonged to the "old order." God and Moses had gotten the Israelites out of Egypt, but they were never able to get the Egypt out of the Israelites—that is, the older generation of Israelites.

God told Moses several times that He wanted to kill off the older generation and raise up a new generation who would be willing to follow Moses into Canaan. But each time, Moses argued with God, insisting that He must preserve the older generation. The end result was that the murmuring old Israelites finally pushed Moses beyond his patience, so that he angrily struck the rock instead of speaking to it according to God's prophetic instructions (Num.20:7-13). Because of Moses' act of impatience, frustration, self-will and disobedience, God cancelled that part of his personal prophecy which said he would go into Canaan.

Lessons to Be Learned. Three biblical truths are manifested in this incident. First, our actions can cancel part of what has been prophesied personally to us, even after much of what was prophesied has already been fulfilled. The fulfillment of all the remaining prophecies in our lives depends on our continual obedience, faith and patience.

The second truth revealed here is that God's grace for endurance does not extend beyond the bounds of God's purpose. When we demand that God do things our way, then we are on our own. He may very well just give us what we want—to our own destruction.

We see this reality, not only in this incident with Moses, but also when the Israelites grumbled about the manna in the wilderness, demanding meat instead. God gave them the thing they craved when He sent quail—but even as they ate the meat, a severe plague broke out and killed many (see Num.11).

In the New Testament as well we read that those who hate truth and insist on harboring falsehood get what they want in the end, to their own doom. The apostle Paul said of such people: "They perish because they refused to love the truth and so be saved. For this reason God sends them a powerful delusion so that they will believe the lie and so that all will be condemned who have not believed the truth but have delighted in wickedness" (2Thes.2:10,11 NIV).

It is best to allow God's prophetic purposes and decrees to prevail rather than nag Him with what we think is a better idea. Remember what happened with King Hezekiah of Israel: When God decreed prophetically through Isaiah that he would die, the king wept bitterly and begged for an extension of his life (see Is.38). In response, God granted Hezekiah fifteen more years. But in those added years, Hezekiah's behavior led to disaster for the nation. Both Hezekiah and the people of Israel would have been much better off if God's original prophetic pronouncement had stood.

The third truth is that pastoral compassion and prophetic purpose will sometimes be at odds, causing friction and even conflict within the local church between pastor and prophet. So a willingness to humbly seek God together to determine His desire for the congregation is critical for maintaining unity in the local church leadership.

From the standpoint of human compassion and a pastor's heart, we might judge Moses' intercession and insistence as commendable. But from a prophetic perspective his action was foolish and futile. It only postponed God's judgments; God still had to kill off almost the entire older generation before He could fulfill His prophetic promise given to Abraham some four centuries before (see Gen.15:16).

We typically praise Moses and blame Saul, yet we fail to recognize that Moses cancelled his prophecy concerning Canaan just as Saul cancelled his prophecy concerning kingship over Israel. Moses was removed as Saul was, and Joshua was raised up to become the new leader of a new generation that entered Canaan. In a similar way today, a

"Davidic company" is replacing the old "Saul order," a "Joshua generation" is replacing the old-order "wilderness generation." They will enter the Church's Canaan to fulfill God's prophetic purpose.

Pastors Today Must Not Be Overprotective. Moses is typical of the prophet who is senior pastor of a congregation. When prophet-shepherds are overprotective of their flock—so mercy-motivated that they will not allow God to chasten properly those under their charge—they set themselves up for Moses' type of prophetic pitfall. Those faithful old-order church members whom "Pastor Mercy" feels so obligated to protect and preserve will eventually cause him or her to sin against God and cancel his or her ultimate prophetic purpose. God will eventually remove that pastor and raise up a new one to take the Joshua generation into the promised Canaan land.

I have heard God say to many pastors in prophecy that some of his or her church's members will not believe and go with His vision for that church. The word of God told those pastors to let such people go and not try to talk them out of leaving. The Lord cannot take people into their promised prophetic ministry unless they will believe and respond properly.

God's purpose is greater than human preferences. It makes no difference whether someone is a founding member of a church who has given thousands of dollars. Prophetic pastors must follow God's divine directives. If instead they are over-protective, too mercy-motivated or bound by a sense of obligation to the old-order portion of their congregations, then they will probably die in the wilderness with those church members and never enter into the present move of God—nor ever fulfill their full prophetic potential.

7

PROPHET JONAH'S PRIDE
AND
JUDGMENT PITFALL

Jonah had the weed seed attitude of pride and a root problem of being too judgmental (see Jonah 1-4). While Moses was motivated too much by mercy, Jonah was motivated too much by judgment. He was more interested in seeing God destroy the wicked than in seeing God have mercy on them. He had the character flaw of being more concerned with his reputation than with the people he ministered to.

Modern-Day Jonahs. Like Jonah, some modern-day prophets grieve more over the loss of their "gourd shade" of personal comfort than they do over the death of thousands of people. Their own spirit is so intertwined with the Johnson grass roots of selfishness, pride, anger, vengeance, self-will and personal ambition that they run from any prophetic assignment that has the possibility of making them look bad or failing to bring them a profit. God must providentially force them to be his spokesmen by putting them into restrictive situations at the bottom of the ocean of life until they are willing to obey. Though the Lord will not make them go against their will, He has ways of making them willing.

They are immature prophets who respond to God and the ministry like spoiled children. They want to dictate to God how to fulfill His word through them because they do not trust God to do it in the way they think it should be done. They try to motivate God by threats and intimidation.

"God," they say, "I'll run away, backslide, quit the ministry [or a dozen other childish things] if you don't do it my way! If I do that for you, then you must do this for me. You owe me, God! This isn't fair; I deserve better than this! I don't have to put up with this, and if you don't treat me better, I won't be your spokesman!"

Jonah Pitfall Leads to Serious Problems. Prophets must beware of the Jonah pitfall. It will get them in serious trouble with God. If we follow in Jonah's footsteps, He will prepare a "great fish" situation to swallow us up and wrap sea weed around our head. God will providentially hold us at the bottom of life in a restricted area until we quit blaming Him and others for our problem and become willing to pay our vows and obey the Lord.

If we persist in maintaining the attitude Jonah had, God will take away the protective covering He has provided for us. He will let the sultry winds blow and the hot sun beat down on our head until we are wishing, as Jonah did, that we were dead.

As Bishop of a company of prophets, I have had to deal with immature prophets who were angry with God's dealings in their lives. They were resentful and murmured when God did not work on their time schedule to come through as they expected. Such childish, spoiled prophets must allow God to mature them to unselfish service, putting to death self-promotion, popularity and all other unChristlike character flaws.

We have no record that God ever used Jonah as a prophet again. He seems to have had no continuing ministry as Isaiah, Elisha, Jeremiah or Daniel did. Prophets who do not root out the problems of anger, pride, selfishness and more concern for themselves than for God's prophetic purpose will become short-lived shooting stars—rather than a permanent planet orbiting around God's eternal purpose. So—like the sailors on the ship to Tarshish discovered—if you find that you have a "Jonah" on board, you had better throw it overboard or risk going down yourself.

Jonah pitfalls - pride judgemental
Childlike/Childish attitude

8

ACHAN AND THE "MY MINISTRY SYNDROME"

The Severity of God's Judgment on Achan. Achan's great sin was to take from the conquered city of Jericho a Babylonian garment, a two-pound bar of gold, and about eight pounds of silver (Joshua 6:17-19; 7:1-26). The sin was serious because God had explicitly declared that all the gold, silver, bronze and iron was devoted to God's treasury. He had further said that if any soldiers took it for themselves, they would be accursed and would incur God's curse on all Israel as well.

Everything, including all humans and animals in Jericho, was to be killed and then destroyed by fire. If any broke God's commandment, they would receive the same judgment decreed for Jericho. Achan did just that, so he and his family and animals were stoned to death by the Israelites, then burned and covered with a heap of stones.

A New Place Is a Dangerous Place. God's severest judgments are manifest when He is establishing His people in a new place of restoration truth and ministry. For that same reason, He struck Ananias and Sapphira dead for being deceitful when He was establishing the New Testament Church (Acts 5:1-11). The Lord's purpose in such severity is to produce the reverential fear of God within the people and to let all know that He is serious about the principles He is establishing for His new movement.

I believe that the current Prophetic movement has brought the Church "across Jordan" in its restoration journey to possess

41

its promised Canaan land. If this is a divinely established fact, then that means judgment has begun with the house of God, and His severity in judging all disobedience has begun to be manifest in the Church since 1988, when the Prophetic movement was birthed. (See "The Beginnings of the Prophetic Movement" in chapter 7 of volume 2 in this series.)

Achan's Character Flaw and Pitfall. What caused Achan to sin as he did when thousands of his fellow Israelite soldiers resisted the temptation? When Joshua asked Achan for his reasons, he replied, "I saw, I coveted, I took, I put it in **my** tent." Clearly, his root problem was selfishness.

Achan was like Christians who are stuck in the seventh chapter of Romans, where the words me, my, myself and I are repeated fifty-two times in twenty-six verses. People in that condition need to move on to Romans chapter eight—from the "self" chapter of their life to the "Spirit" chapter—where the Godhead is mentioned fifty-seven times in thirty-nine verses, and there are only two first-person pronouns. When you take the "I" out of SIN and reduce it to zero it becomes "SON". True sonship in Jesus Christ is accomplished by us dying to self and allowing the life of Christ to be made manifest in our mortal bodies (2Cor.4:10-11; Gal.2:20).

If we fail to move on to chapter eight, then we will end up praying the prayer that Paul prayed at the end of chapter seven: "Oh, wretched man that I am! who shall deliver me from the body [self-oriented life] of this death?" (Rom.7:24).

"My Ministry Syndrome." This is the character flaw I call the "My Ministry Syndrome." Achan's weed seed attitude was selfishness and concern only for "me and mine" with no concern for others with similar needs and opportunities. Achan was self-promoting and possessive without regard for directions given by the leadership. He was a loner without the team ministry concept.

The other 600,000 soldiers had also spent time in the wilderness (parallel to our preparation for ministry); made sacrifices (times of financial lack and small offerings); gone without change of raiment (lack of new ministry opportunities); and avoided the temptation to grab the gold and silver (bigger offerings or salary). They had endured the same apprenticeship training for warfare in the desert. Even Joshua, the commander-in-chief, did not manifest a presumptuous attitude as Achan did. Nor did Caleb, who had twice as many years of ministry.

The Achan syndrome will make people feel they are exempt from divine directives and have special privileges to enjoy the material things on which God has placed restrictions. When prophets start thinking they deserve more recognition and offerings, or focus only on their own desires, possessions and ministry, then the seed of the Achan spirit is in their heart. When they press for personal promotion, take the gold that belongs to God's treasury and put it in their own "tent" (ministry), then the destructive Johnson grass roots have intertwined with the roots of their good cornstalk.

When Christians lose the greater vision for the success of the whole Body of Christ, then the Achan seed has sprouted into a plant of self-destruction. They have taken of the accursed thing that God hates—the pride, selfishness and self-promotion that caused the fall of God's heavenly minister of music, Lucifer (Is.14:12-15).

God's Overall Purpose Our Primary Goal. We who are prophets must constantly remind ourselves that our primary goal should be the fulfillment of God's overall purpose for His Church, not our possessing the most or making our ministry the greatest. For example, Christ's purpose for my particular ministry as an individual prophet is to fulfill His greater purpose in raising up a last-days company of prophets. This international company is then called to the greater purpose of co-laboring with Christ to fulfill God's plans for His universal Church. Christ's Church is then called to co-labor with God in fulfilling His purposes for planet earth. And the perfected Church on the redeemed earth is destined to fulfill that even greater eternal purpose which God purposed in Christ Jesus, the Lord of heaven and earth.

Most all of the root problems of ministers and other church members would be eliminated if we had the proper perspective on God's purpose for our position in the Body of Christ. The apostle Paul portrayed this truth when he used the analogy of the human body to describe the Church, declaring, "Now ye are the Body of Christ, and members in particular" (1Cor.12:27). Though there are many members, there is only one Body with one overall purpose.

Interdependent, Not Independent. For that reason, each member has the responsibility to fulfill its own function and to stay properly related to the Head, Jesus Christ. The ministry and success of any individual member is not an end in itself; rather, it exists to contribute to the function and fulfillment of the whole Body. And the whole Body was formed and now functions to fulfill the desires and directives of its Head.

We are not independent ministries, but interdependent upon one another and upon the Body's headship directives. If we have the old perspective that insists the prophet is a loner, functioning independently of the rest of the Church, then we are subject to the pitfall of selfishness. The banana separated from the bunch is the one that gets peeled and eaten. The lone sheep gets devoured by the wolves.

If the prophetic ministry is the eye or the mouth of the Body, then it cannot say to the hand or foot, "I don't need you." The Body may be able to function without certain members, but no member can function apart from the Body. A member that gets separated from the Body withers and dies unless it is put on some sort of artificial life support system.

But God is now in the process of pulling the plug on the support system of every ministry that is not properly related within the Body of Christ. Every member of the Body diseased with the cancerous cells of exclusiveness, seclusiveness and independence will be surgically removed by God. The root system of the "my ministry and my needs first" syndrome will be plowed upside down and exposed for what it is, then raked and burned in God's purifying fire (see Mal.3:1-3; 1Cor.3:12-15).

The Achan spirit manifests itself when ministers become so wrapped up in their own needs, desires and ministry that they think they have the right to take special privileges and possessions beyond that of their fellow ministers. Such a spirit is a seed of self-deception that will cause ministers to become a law unto themselves, with an attitude that insists, "I deserve greater offerings and more opportunities. If I don't take, I won't get. If I don't promote my own ministry, no one else will." We must not let the enemy come during the night of temptation and sow such Achan seeds in the field of our hearts (see Matt.13:24-26).

9

JUDAS' CHARACTER FLAWS:
"DESIRE TO BE REWARDED FOR EVERY SERVICE"

Judas and Achan had a kindred spirit and the same root problem. Judas' outward sin was the betrayal of his friend when he sold Jesus out to the enemy. But the thinking and attitude that caused Judas to take this action was the root problem. I am quite familiar with the problem, because in my years as bishop of the Christian International Network of Prophetic Ministers (CI—NPM), I have had occasion to counsel and deal with some "Judas" ministers with a similar character flaw.

Disappointment in Personal Ambitions. Judging from what I have seen in these cases, Judas' thoughts probably went something like this: "I've forsaken my business and sacrificed my opportunities to advance myself in position and possessions over the last three years by following Jesus day and night. Now I get the impression from what Jesus is saying and doing that He won't fulfill my dream. I thought following Jesus would advance my position, power and prestige, but I was wrong."

In this way Judas probably built up in his own mind a case for feeling justified in taking the actions he did. He began to interpret and apply the prophetic promises Jesus had made to the Twelve in a way that was different from the Lord's intent (such as Christ's words that they would sit on thrones with Him, ruling the twelve tribes of Israel, Matt.19:28).

It looked to Judas as if Jesus had misled him and would not fulfill His word to them. So he probably reasoned, "I could have made at least thirty pieces of silver profit during these past three years. I deserve something for the years of sacrifice and service I have given to Jesus."

Steps in Satan's Deception. Satan's first step in developing the Judas spirit in people is to convince them that the leadership they have been serving, and to whom they have been related and accountable, are not living up to the promises they have made to them. These "promises" may even be personal prophecies they received or prophecies they once heard the leadership give to the church or ministry as a group. The people who are disappointed in this way typically make a private (and wrong) interpretation and application of the leader's promises or prophetic statements that lead them to conclude the leaders have not fulfilled their word.

Such Judas type of thinking allows a sense of self-justification for betraying friendship and selling out to the enemy for personal gain. This action consequently makes those who take it feel judged by others for what they have done. So self-deception must then come to convince them that the leadership and others are neither understanding nor beneficial.

Pride and an exalted sense of self-importance come next to convince them to do what Lucifer did—to pull away and head up their own ministry. They leave the fellowship and refuse to allow their overseer to have input into their lives. By then, the spirit of self-delusion has invented a dozen arguments why they are "justified" in their every attitude and action. "Every way of a man is right in his own eyes," says Proverbs, "but the Lord pondereth the hearts" (Prov.21:2).

The Judas spirit starts in seed form with the feeling that we must be rewarded immediately for every service rendered and given recognition or a higher position for time and money spent to participate in and propagate the ministry. It begins with the attitude that says, "God owes me for services rendered. I deserve better. I deserve more offerings and honor than I am receiving. They should recognize me and have me speak more often." This is where it starts; but if we do not allow God and the leaders over us to correct this character flaw and adjust this attitude, we will hang ourselves ministerially just as surely as Judas hung himself on a tree.

No Rights to Self-Promotion or Self-Preservation. Prophets must take on the ministry attitude of the Spirit of Christ, which does not demand the right of self-promotion and self-preservation. Jesus did not demand that the Father promote Him and give Him a good reputation. Instead, Jesus made Himself of no reputation (Phil.2:7). He could have called for an angelic host to help Him (Matt.26:53), but He laid down His rights and His life for His brethren. He let others hang Him on a tree. Yet this seeming act of self-destruction actually led to His preservation, because the Father raised Him from the dead and promoted His ministry to the right hand of the throne of heaven.

Jesus was dealing with this weed seed attitude in His disciples when He declared that "except a corn of wheat fall into the ground and die, it abideth alone: but if it die, it bringeth forth much fruit" (John 12:24). Prophets must die to self-ambition, self-promotion and self-interest. For if they don't allow the "death to self" process to take place, they are destined eventually to sell out their relationship with Jesus, as Judas did, for the sake of worldly goods and carnal desires.

The bottom line is this: Selfishness is the root problem of ninety-nine percent of all unscriptural attitudes and actions. Self-centeredness is what gives power to the three sources of all sin—the lust of the flesh, the lust of the eyes, and the pride of life (1John 2:16). All outward sins come from one of these three sources, and they receive their right and power to function in an individual through his or her unsanctified self-life.

That's why in dealing with prophetic pitfalls, we must lay the axe of truth to the root of the tree rather than wasting our time merely pruning back the branches. The self life out of order is the root of the tree; individual sins, the breaking of the Ten Commandments with the works of the flesh, are simply the branches of the tree. Or to use our earlier illustration, adultery, lying, dishonesty, anger and other sinful manifestations are the blades of the "Johnson grass" growing above ground. But selfishness is the root system underground. We may cut away the blades of grass, but they will grow back again and again until the underlying root system is destroyed.

Peter faced circumstances similar to those of Judas. He left his fishing business and his family to follow Jesus. When Jesus was arrested, he also became discouraged, disillusioned and confused, even to the point of denying His leader and Lord. Yet Peter repented when he realized he had spoken foolishly and immaturely and had acted wrongly toward Jesus. Like the prodigal son in Jesus' parable, he turned away from the attitude that says **give me** wealth, fame and freedom, and took on instead the attitude that says **make me** a servant to my Father.

We all have said and done or will someday say and do foolish things under great pressure, fear and confusion, especially when—like the Twelve—we see all our hopes, dreams and ministry falling apart all around us. When that happens, do we follow the example of Peter or of Judas? Like Peter, we must be willing to admit wrongdoing and then change. If we become divinely flexible and adjustable, God can restore us and cause our ministry to become more effective than we ever dreamed possible.

10

JAMES AND JOHN SYNDROME

Most New Testament historians estimate that James and John were in their early twenties when Jesus chose them to be two of His special disciples and eventually two of His twelve apostles. After following Jesus for three years, James and John asked Jesus to grant them a request (see Mk.10:35-41). When Jesus asked what they wanted Him to do, they said: "Grant unto us that we may sit, one on thy right hand, and the other on thy left hand, in thy glory."

In response, Jesus did not rebuke the brothers, but simply asked them whether they were able to drink of the cup of suffering and death that He would drink. They assured Him they could, and Jesus answered, in effect, "You will! But right now I cannot grant your request or assure you that position even if you follow me to the death."

More Zeal than Wisdom. James and John exemplify the weed seed attitude of desire for position and power rather than servanthood and ministry to others. The James and John syndrome is the immature, ambitious drive that causes people to go to the leadership asking for the ministry that is highest and most closely related to the leader. You see, these two brothers were not content to be called simply among the Twelve. They wanted to be exalted and to have special privileges and positions above their fellow apostles.

James and John portray the root problem of a young prophetic minister who has more zeal than wisdom. They desired self-promotion and privileged positions above their peers without understanding the greater price that had to be paid. Part of that price would be death to selfish ambition for position and continual conformity to the character of Jesus Christ.

Jesus did not rebuke the brothers for their desire to be close to Him in His glory. He just responded to that desire with teaching about serving verses mastering, ministering verses managing, and greatness and authority in God's kingdom verses the world's standard for authority and greatness. Out of the "10 M's," they had the "M" of motive out of order. Their motivations had yet to be purified and sanctified.

Keep in mind that these disciples had enjoyed the benefit of three years of listening to Jesus' teaching on the principles of the Kingdom. They had watched a living demonstration by Jesus of how His followers were to minister. We might have thought that with such training, they would have understood Jesus sufficiently to forego such an immature request.

Nevertheless, James and John still showed a weed seed attitude, and we can expect that many other young (and not-so-young) ministers today will do the same. So we who are in a leadership role of developing other ministers must pray for the patience, wisdom and prophetic insight of Jesus when dealing with young men and women who manifest the James and John syndrome.

God's Scaffolding. I must confess that I had this syndrome in the early years of my own ministry. The accompanying ambition and drive were a help in some ways, but God had to take that from me before He could make my ministry what He wanted it to be. It was a scaffolding that kept me going until God could lay the permanent stones of **His** motives, ambitions and character.

All young, ambitious prophets and apostles must recognize the truth that the man or woman must be made before the mighty ministry, message and miracles. Joshua and Elisha, for example, each completed years of apprenticeship serving another man's vision and ministry before they received great authority and recognition in their own ministry.

As a bishop I continually pray that God will grant me the divine wisdom to discern between those with the Judas and Achan spirit and those with the James and John spirit. My compassion goes out to those who have a pure heart yet are ignorant and immature in some of the things they say and do. But my fatherly concern for the ministers I am developing causes a righteous indignation to rise up within me against the Judas and Achan spirit.

Resist the Temptation to Feel Like a Failure. At the same time, I want to encourage other ministerial leaders not to be intimidated by a sense of failure when their disciples fail to manifest in their lives the fruit of what they have been taught, like James and John; or who deny them and turn away from them for a while, like Peter; or who even turn against them for personal gain and help others "crucify" them as Judas did to Jesus. If even God the Father lost His minister of music, Lucifer, and if even Jesus lost his disciple and treasurer, Judas, then we should not be too discouraged if we have a similar experience.

Today we read in the Bible about the apostles Peter, James and John, who became pillars of the early Church. These were the mighty apostles, full of wisdom and maturity, that all the rest of the Church looked to as leadership. So it is hard from our vantage point to grasp the reality that in their pre-Pentecost days, these three made more mistakes and caused Jesus more problems than all the rest. They were immature, self-promoting and ambitious in those early days of their training for the apostolic ministry.

Keeping their example in mind, we can conclude that there is hope for today's young apostles and prophets who have a true heart for Christ but presently also have drive and ambition for greatness. We who have been in the ministry more than twenty years may cringe inside when we see their immaturity, but we must ask God to grant us grace, patience and wisdom to help them grow.

Jesus called James and John His "sons of thunder." Like other Christian leaders, I too have my "sons of thunder." My hope and expectation is that they will become pillars and propagators of the Prophetic movement just as James and John were in the New Testament Church.

We should note here that Matthew tells how Salome, the mother of James and John, originally hatched the idea to have them ask for special positions, and she pushed for the request to be made (Matt.20:20-28). Ministers must be especially careful of those family members and fellow ministers who are over-zealous for their success, promotion and recognition. Such relatives can cause ministers to do foolish and immature things that will put them in precarious positions and cause friction and resentment in relationships with other ministers.

We must practice in our own ministries the biblical principle that declares a person's gift will make room for him or her (Pr.18:16) and that mature ministry will manifest itself, because promotion comes from the Lord (Ps.75:6,7). At the same time, we must have patience with those who show the James and John spirit. Pastors, bishops and apostolic overseers need the chance to work with those who manifest this spirit until it becomes clear whether they will mature over time.

11

PROPHET BALAAM PITFALLS

The prophet Balaam should be thoroughly studied by every prophet who wants to avoid the flaws that biblical character showed (see Num.22:1-24:25; 31:8-16; Deut.23:5,6; Josh. 13:22, 24:9,10; Micah 6:5). Balaam could give a true word of the Lord, yet he became a false prophet in his personal attitude and way of life. His example should teach us that judging the prophet and judging the prophetic word are two different matters.

Prophecy Judged in Three Areas. We must judge the content of a prophecy in three areas. First, its spiritual message must conform to biblical truth. Second, objective, verifiable statements about the past and present can be checked against the facts. And third, predictions for the future are judged by whether they come to pass.

On the other hand, we must judge the prophet or prophetess in a different way. True and false prophetic ministers are discerned by their character, the spirit of wisdom, the fruit of the Holy Spirit in their personal lives, and the fruit of their ministry that remains after the initial manifestations of miracles or other signs.

As we read all the scriptural references to Balaam throughout the Bible, we find several pitfalls and character flaws. To his credit, we must note that he held to one important prophetic rule: He refused to prophesy anything except what God had given him to say. In fact, he even declared to Balak that he could prophesy no differently even if he gave him half his kingdom and great positions. Yet Balaam was nevertheless ambitious for fame, fortune and prestige.

Some "M's" in Order, Some Not. Evidently, though Balaam had some of his "Ten M's" in order, he had enough of them out of order to cause him to be judged a false prophet by Jesus (Rev.2:14), Peter (2Pet.2:15,16) and Jude (Jude 11) in the New Testament. His "M's" of message, ministry, manhood and morality appear to have been in order, but his "M's" of motive, maturity, methods and money were not. Though he was committed to speaking nothing but pure words from the Lord, yet he was self-determined and lusted enough for power and possession to persist in hoping that God would allow him to prophesy something that Balak would reward.

God told Balaam when he first inquired that he was not to go with Balak to curse Israel. After further offers of reward, however, Balaam inquired again of God to see if there were not some way he could go. God told Balaam that he could go if the men came for him again. Yet there is no indication in the scriptural text that this confirmation came before Balaam saddled up his donkey to go to Balak to prophesy against Israel.

A Self-Willed Prophet Takes a Mile When God Gives an Inch. God was angered because Balaam went ahead anyhow. He sent an angel to cause a breakdown in the prophet's transportation so that he would be stopped. The donkey saw God's angel of providential restriction, but the prophet Balaam was too blinded by his self-will to see that God was involved in his frustrating situation.

A Point for Prophets to Ponder. Judging from Balaam's story, even a donkey can discern the spiritual world and God's divine restrictions better than a prophet blinded by lust for riches, power and promotion. Prophets with the character flaws of

Balaam allow the potential rewards of riches to influence them toward displeasing God in their striving to please people for earthly gain.

Balaam tried to please God and serve Mammon at the same time. He had the root problem that Paul calls the root of all evil, the love of money (1Tim.6:10). I believe Balaam held a secret resentment in his heart toward Jehovah for not allowing him to prophesy anything that Balak desired against Israel—thus causing him to lose all of Balak's promised riches and promotion.

Balaam could not prophesy anything except what God told him. But he finally by-passed that restriction by not prophesying in the name of Jehovah. Instead, he pulled upon his prophetic insight and gave counsel to the Moabites and Midianites about how they could destroy the Israelites by causing them to sin against God by adultery and idolatry (Rev.2:14). By doing so, Balaam finally received the riches and position he wanted, but he was also destroyed with the Midianites under the judgment of God (Josh.13:22).

Seeing Prophets As God Sees Them. When we read the account of Balaam in Numbers, he does not look like a false or wrongly motivated prophet. Only in light of Peter's, Jude's and Jesus' comments about Balaam do we begin to see him as God saw him. If we were to judge this prophet only by the accuracy of his prophecies, we would have to declare him a true prophet.

Balaam prophesied only what God spoke to him even though he was offered great riches to prophesy differently. The references in Numbers make him look like a man of integrity in the prophetic ministry who resisted all temptations. In fact, he gives the only Messianic prophecy in the book of Numbers, and he was the greatest prophet among his peers.

So on what basis does the New Testament declare him to be a false prophet? His false status is only perceived by God's spirit of discernment, which searches the heart and motive. The

Scriptures declare that human beings judge by outward looks and performances, but God judges the heart, weighs the spirit and identifies the motive behind the performance (1Sam.16:7; Prov.16:2).

Motive Plus Action Equals Deed. The book of Revelation says that every person's eternal reward and destiny will be determined by his or her deeds. Deeds are more than actions; they are formed by the equation I call "M + A = D"—that is, Motive plus Action equals Deed. So in judging whether someone is a true or false prophet, God evaluates the person's motive as well as ministry.

Several incidents recorded in Scripture show people who seem to be right nevertheless giving false prophecies and then being judged as false prophets. But Balaam is the only one who portrays the reality that a prophet can give accurate prophecies and yet be a wrong enough person on the inside to be judged a false prophet. Sadly enough, most Christians would not realize that a Balaam prophet is a false prophet. Most of them only know the passage in Deuteronomy (18:22) that declares a person's "true prophet" status is determined by whether the word that person gives is accurate and comes to pass.

Balaam spoke only God-directed words, and they came to pass. But the New Testament uses him as an example of what a prophet should **not** be and do. God is more concerned about the purity of His prophets than the accuracy of their prophecies; He values the men and women themselves and their motives as well as their message and ministry.

Wolves in Sheep's Clothing. Listen to the words of Jesus concerning inward spirit and motivation: "Beware of false prophets which come to you in sheep's clothing, but inwardly they are ravening wolves. Ye shall know them by their fruits....Not everyone that saith unto me, Lord, Lord, shall enter into the kingdom of heaven: but he that doeth the will of my Father which is in heaven. Many will say to me in that day, Lord, Lord, have we not prophesied in thy name? and in thy name have cast out devils? and in thy name done many wonderful works? And then will I profess unto them, I never knew you: depart from me, ye that work iniquity" (Matt.7:15,16,21-23).

Jesus said a prophet can have the outward clothing and ministry of a sheep but the inward spirit and motivation of a wolf. These are prophets with accurate prophecies and miraculous works, but they are not righteous—not right inside.

Intimate with God. The verb "to know" is used in the Hebrew of the Old Testament to convey the intimate relationship between husband and wife, as in "Adam knew his wife Eve" (Gen.4:1). I think Jesus' use of the word "know" here conveys a similar meaning in a metaphorical sense.

When speaking of these false prophets, Jesus says that at one time, they went through the spiritual "legal ceremony" of being married to Him by being born again and called to the ministry. They took the power of attorney of their "husband" (Christ) and wrote checks on the bank of heaven, signing it with the name of Jesus. Now they prophesy and work wonderful works by God's grace, faith and divine enablements. But they never allow Jesus' life and motive to become their motivation and purpose for ministry. So on that day, Jesus will say to them that He never **knew** them.

Prophetic ministers must guard against self-deception, self-justification and improper motivation. So we need others to help us see ourselves in areas where we have blind spots. The book of Proverbs tells us that "all the ways of a man are clean in his own eyes" (Pr.16:2), and the prophet Jeremiah said, "The heart is deceitful above all things, and desperately wicked; who can know it?" (Jer.17:9).

For that reason, every prophet needs to submit to someone whom he or she respects enough to be willing to listen when the other person provides instruction and correction. That is why in the CI-NPM we have established a structure of accountability: the senior apostolic prophet with the vision and burden for prophetic ministers serves as president, and then a board of governors consisting of anointed and mature apostles, prophets and pastors serves as part of the headship and as a place of accountability and relationship for all the ministers in the network.

At the same time, as bishop of the network I am personally accountable to my fellow bishops in the International College of Charismatic Bishops. Most of them are older than I am and have been in the ministry longer, so they are in a good position to bring correction and reveal blind spots in my life.

12

JOSEPH'S DIVINE OPTIMISM
VS.
JACOB'S HUMAN PESSIMISM

The biblical characters of Joseph and Jacob provide us with a useful study in contrasts with regard to their attitude toward life and ministry. In their stories we find that Jacob's root problem of a pessimistic personality hinders ministry, while Joseph's perspective and principles of life can preserve a minister through difficult times. So we want to avoid the pitfalls of the former and imitate the example of the latter.

Jacob's Negativism. Jacob is typical of the present-day prophet with a persecution complex and a negative attitude toward people and the ministry (see Gen.42:36; 47:9). He had to leave home because of conflict with his father and older brother. This is typical of the prophetic minister who has had to leave his or her denomination or home church over conflict with denominational leaders or a local pastor.

After he left home, Jacob's conflicts continued. He worked under his uncle Laban, a man who constantly tried to use him, deceive him and manipulate him into building his own kingdom. Jacob had to outwit and manipulate Laban in order to survive and prosper.

When Jacob met God and was transformed, he ceased his manipulating methods. But he retained a negative attitude. Every time something unpleasant happened to him, he concluded, "All things are against me" (Gen.47:9).

Prophetic ministers with a background and personality like Jacob's will continually have to overcome the feeling that others are trying to use them or are working against them. Every tragedy or setback brings a response of pessimism, discouragement, self-pity and complaining, with periods of non-productivity.

Joseph's Positive Perspective. On the other hand, prophets with the Joseph perspective have an overall view of God's eternal purpose. They never lose faith in the Lord's original communication with them about His purpose for their lives.

Joseph believed everything that happened to him was providentially ordained by God. He declared to His brothers: "Not you, but God sent me to Egypt; you meant all that you did to me for evil, but God meant it to me for good" (see Gen.45:5-8, 50:20).

Joseph's New Testament counterpart in this regard, the apostle Paul, had the same perspective. Paul declared: "We know that all things work together for good to them that love God, to them who are the called according to his purpose" (Rom.8:28).

Prophets with the Joseph personality believe as he did that God is providentially directing all the affairs of their lives as they seek to do His will and fulfill His purpose. They forgive quickly those who have used and abused them. They even bless such people when they repent, allowing their former persecutors to share in God's prosperity and promotion in their lives.

Personal "Earthquakes." My wife and I have endured four major "Joseph" setbacks over the course of our years in the ministry. These are what I describe as mind-blowing, heartbreaking, soul-shaking, seemingly world-ending situations. Though I won't go into details in describing our experiences, I think it may be helpful in speaking to younger ministers to take the approach Paul did in writing to the Corinthian church when he reminded them of the trials he had endured (2Cor.4:8-10, 11:23-33).

In the past I have been persecuted, lied about, dismissed from ministry, deprived of ministerial positions and opportunities without just cause, and left to derive income from the secular world for years until God opened again the doors to full-time ministry. I have been accused of believing and teaching doctrines that are actually foreign to me, and I have been accused of wrong purpose and motives for ministering. I have also been accused a couple of times of being a false prophet and delivering inaccurate words.

No wonder, then, that I can readily identify with Joseph, who was resented, cast out and sold into slavery by his brothers. And you can be assured the devil and the flesh have tried to tempt me to yield to the Jacob type of pessimism. But the word of God leaves no room for ministers and other saints to become bitter, resentful, vengeful, unforgiving or pessimistic—no matter how cruel, heartless, unscriptural, unethical and unfair someone's behavior toward us might have been.

My wife and I have lived through four major personal "earthquakes" that would probably register over eight on the spiritual Richter scale in measuring their severity. And we have weathered countless other minor tremors. Yet we survived them all by maintaining Joseph's good seed attitude and the apostle Paul's positive faith perspective that insists God works providentially through all things in the lives of those who love Him and are called according to His purpose (Rom.8:28).

I would strongly exhort all prophetic ministers to develop the same attitude and principles. The **true** prophet's spirit and personality profile demonstrates forgiveness, lovingkindness, restoration and service to the Body of Christ. Those who minister out of a heart of negativism, pessimism and wounded hurts from the past will not experience progress or promotion to new positions.

Be Open to Correction. If someone should counsel you that you are manifesting any of the hindrances to growth we have discussed in this section—whether weed seed attitudes, root problems, syndromes or character flaws—respond with the wisdom from above that is receptive and teachable (James 3:17). The book of Proverbs tells us how to be a wise prophetic minister:

> The wise also will hear and increase in learning, and the person of understanding will acquire skill and attain to godly counsel so that he may be able to steer his course rightly.... Reprove not a scorner, lest he hate you; reprove a wise man, and he will love you. Give instruction to a wise man and he will be yet wiser; teach a righteous man [one upright and in right standing with God] and he will increase with learning (Pr.1:5;9:8,9 AMP).

The main character flaw of scorners and fools described in Proverbs is that in their eyes, correction means rejection. For that reason, when you try to correct scornful or foolish prophets, they feel you are against them and out to hinder or destroy them. So even correction given in love with great tactfulness by delegated authority is almost impossible for them to hear, receive and act upon in the spirit of wisdom.

We certainly do not want to be in the company of scorners and fools. So we should prayerfully consider any suggestion we may receive concerning a need for adjustment if we want to avoid all the devil's pitfalls for prophets and the personal character flaws that could ultimately destroy us and our ministry. We must dedicate ourselves to exemplify the true spirit and character of the great company of prophets God is raising up to make ready a people and to prepare the way for Christ's coming.

The Biblical characters used in this section to portray many of the prophet syndromes, character flaws, root problems and weed seed attitudes are but a small portion of that which could be portrayed. Like the writer of the book of Hebrews in giving his list of the heroes of the faith concluded by saying, ... "the time would fail me to tell of Gideon, Barak, Samson, Jephthah, David, Samuel and of the prophets" (Heb.11:32). Future volumes will cover the Jezebel spirit, Absalom syndrome, David's success syndrome resulting in him committing adultery and murder, plus many others who manifested certain character flaws that hindered their walk with the Lord.

Hopefully, what has been presented will give the reader keys to open the door into the inner rooms of hidden motives and root problems. May God grant each of us the wisdom and grace to deal with each of these weed seeds before they sprout and become trees of unrighteousness.

10 M's

for

Maturing & Maintaining Manhood & Ministry
Determining Prophetic Ministers True/False Status

1. MANHOOD

Gen.1:26,27	God makes a man before manifesting mighty ministry
Rom.8:29	Man-apart from position, message or ministry
Heb.2:6,10	Per-son-al-ity-evaluating person not performance
1Tim.2:5	Jesus-manhood 30 years; ministry 3 1/2; 10 to 1 ratio

2. MINISTRY

2Cor.6:3	No offense to ministry; 1Cor.2:4,5 - power & demonstration
Mt.7:15-21	By their fruits you shall know them - anointing, results
Deut.18:22	Prophecies or preaching productive - proven, pure, positive

3. MESSAGE

Eph.4:15	Speak the truth in love; present-truth, and life giving
1Tim.4:2	Message balanced, scriptural, doctrinally and spiritually right
Mk.16:20	God confirms His Word - not person, pride or reputation

4. MATURITY

Jas.3:17	Attitude right; mature in human relations; heavenly wisdom
Gal.5:22	Fruit of spirit, Christlike character, dependable, steadfast, Heb.5:14
1Cor.13	Not childish; Biblically knowledgeable and mature—not a novice.

5. MARRIAGE

1Tim.3:2,5	Scripturally in order. Personal family vs. God's family
1Pet.3:1,7	Priorities straight - God 1st, wife & family, then ministry
Eph.5:22-23	Marriage to exemplify relationship of Christ & His Church

6. METHODS

Tit.1:16	Rigidly righteous, ethical, honest, integrity - upright
Rom.1:18	Not manipulating or deceptive, doesn't speak "evangelastically"
Rom.3:7-8	Good end results do not justify unscriptural methods

7. MANNERS

Tit.1:7;3:1,2	Unselfish, polite, kind, gentleman or lady, discreet
Eph.4:29;5:4	Proper speech and communication in words and mannerism

8. MONEY

1Tim.3:6AMP	"Craving wealth and resorting to ignoble and dishonest methods"
1Tim.6:5-17	Luke 12:15 - Love of money and materialism destroys (i.e. Achan)

9. MORALITY

1Cor.6:9-18	Virtuous, pure and proper relationships, Col.3:5
Eph.5:3	Biblical sexual purity in attitude & action, 1Cor.5:11
Mt.5:28	Wrong thoughts with desire to do - without opportunity to act

10. MOTIVE

Mt.6:1	To serve or to be seen? Fulfill personal drive or God's desire?
1Cor.16:15	True motivation?...To minister or to be a Minister?
Pr.16:2	To herald the truth or just to be heard by man?
1Cor.13:1-3	Motivated by God's love or lust for power, fame, name, etc.

13

THE 10 "M'S"
FOR
MATURING AND MAINTAINING MINISTRY
AND
DISCERNING TRUE AND FALSE MINISTERS

The personal character of a prophetic minister—or of any minister, for that matter—is the foundation of his or her ministry. In recent years we have seen all too clearly that even those Christians whose ministries may have all the so-called signs of "success," such as financial prosperity, international fame and popularity, and even signs following, are doomed to a humiliating collapse if they fail to build their works on a solid base of personal purity and maturity.

In that light, then, before we deal with issues specifically related to prophetic ministry, we need to take a close look at what I have established as "the 10 M's for maturing and maintaining ministry." These are ten areas of our personal lives that need examination and correction if we are to prove ourselves to be true prophetic ministers of God.

1. MANHOOD (OR WOMANHOOD). God created humankind in His own image (Gen.1:26,27). I believe that when the Eternal created Adam, He made him with the kind of body that He wanted His Son to dwell in for eternity. He gave Adam and Eve power to reproduce after their own kind, and He planned that four thousand years down the road, a woman descendant of theirs would be overshadowed by the Holy Spirit to conceive Jesus, who was God in the flesh. Jesus was born with a mortal human body that portrayed God the Father to the world. The Son of God's mortal body died on the cross and shed its life's blood for the redemption of humankind. That human body was placed in a grave but God resurrected and immortalized it. That same body was taken to heaven and seated at the right hand of the Father. That human body is now the eternal body of God the Son forevermore. Christ thus became a God-Man—humanity's perfect God and God's perfect man.

With Jesus in mind as the pattern, God had to make Adam and Eve first in His own image and likeness before they could perform their "ministry" in the garden of Eden. The same is true of us: God wants to make us like Jesus before we can minister as Jesus did. God must make the man or woman before He manifests through him or her a mighty ministry.

I remember how years ago, when I was preaching one night, I was telling the congregation that we must be like God. I meant, of course, that we are to be godly, to be holy, to have the moral character of God. But in that moment as I spoke, I heard the Holy Spirit say, "If you put it that way, the people will despair; they'll think of God the Father, and they know they can't be eternal, all-powerful or all-knowing. Instead, tell them to be like Jesus, the perfect man and the perfect God."

The Church Race. We aren't destined to become God, as New Age teaching would have it. But we are predestined to be conformed to the image of Christ Jesus (Rom.8:29). God created the man Adam to be the father of the whole human race. Abraham was called to be the father of the Hebrew race. But Jesus came to be the spiritual father of a new race of humankind called the "Church race."

This race of people on earth have eternal life in their spirits while their physical bodies are still mortal. At the end of the Church age, all the members of this Church race will have their bodies transformed into eternally immortal bodies. Such a transformation will not change them into any other creature other than human beings, but they will be human beings as God first intended for them to be.

The resurrection-translation of the saints will make their bodies as eternal as their spirits are now. The same Spirit that raised Jesus from the dead will make their physical bodies as immortal as His. Though the Church race of humankind is destined to be spiritual citizens of heaven, yet they will have immortal flesh-and-bone bodies—bodies like the one Jesus now has seated at the right hand of God (Phil.3:21).

God made humanity in the garden of Eden the way He wanted the race to be throughout eternity: with a spirit, soul, and body conformed to God's own image and likeness. God never intended for humankind to evolve into angels, cherubim, seraphim or God Himself. We as saints will never become angels or God, but we will be like the perfect man, Christ Jesus.

Why should we ever want to be anything else? The human being is the highest being God ever created on earth or anywhere in the universe. Blood-washed, redeemed humankind is destined to be joint heirs with Jesus Christ of all that God has (Rom.8:17). There is no higher calling in the universe than to be a new-creation member of the eternal Church race.

Jesus exhorted His followers not to rejoice in the spiritual power and apostolic ministry He had given them, but to be glad that they were God's people with their names written in the Lamb's book of life (Luke 10:20). Paul received this truth and demonstrated it by not boasting in his position as an apostle or in his power to cast out demons and heal the sick. Instead, he boasted in the greater calling of being changed "from glory to glory" until he reached Christ's image and likeness (2Cor.3:18).

Our highest calling and most important goal is not to be the greatest apostle, prophet or prophetic person, but rather to be Christ's type of man or woman that God wants us to be both now and forever. Humankind was made the way it's supposed to be to fulfill God's will and do God's work throughout eternity. Redeemed human beings have the highest calling and greatest destiny of any of God's creation.

Make Christlike Character Your Aim. For us to be godly—that is, like God—means for us to be like Jesus, who is our perfect pattern as believers and as ministers. That means we must be fully human as well—not what I call a "spooky spiritual" weirdo, but rather God's type of man or woman, who knows how to walk in a natural way on the earth while walking in a supernatural way in the Spirit. Our flesh and bone bodies are not sinful for when cleansed by the blood of Jesus and sanctified by the Holy Spirit they become the very dwelling place of God here on planet Earth (1Cor.6:19-20).

Paul told the church at Corinth: "Follow after charity, and desire spiritual gifts" (1Cor.14:1). I believe that the best definition of charity is mature, Christlike character. So one way to paraphrase this verse would be: "Follow after Christlike character at the same time as you desire and activate spiritual gifts." Even as we pursue a goal of ministry through spiritual gifts and activities, we must remember that the overarching goal is character.

Another translation says, "Make love your aim." We must make Christ's character our primary aim, our ultimate goal as we minister. When Paul was telling the Romans about God's ultimate intention for us, he didn't talk about our position, our message, or our ministry. He spoke instead of our character: "For whom he did foreknow, he also did predestinate to be conformed to the image of his Son, that he might be the firstborn among many brethren" (Rom.8:29). Our transformation into Christ's image is what God is primarily after, so whatever happens to us, it is working together for our good toward that goal (Rom.8:28).

In the ultimate purpose of God, then, there are no "good" times or "bad" times for those who love God and are called according to His purpose. The "bad" time you are going through just now may well be the best time for your eternal gain, because it may be doing the most to move you toward the goal of becoming like Jesus. The tough times for the "outer man"—your physical, emotional, financial, and social being—may well be strengthening your "inner man", your spiritual being (2Cor.4:16).

After all, if we are honest, we must admit that we tend to grow the least when everything is going smoothly. Our years of preparation for mature manhood and womanhood are more important than our years of ministry. For without proper personal preparation, our mighty ministry performances will become perverted and cannot permanently endure.

Over the years, I now see, my enemies have taught me more than my friends. Through them, I have learned much wisdom, forgiveness, patience, longsuffering, and understanding of human nature. From an ultimate standpoint, Christians don't have problems; we only have predestinated purposes ordained by God to conform us to the image of Christ.

Since the scripture declares that Jesus Himself was made perfect through suffering (Heb.2:10), how can we expect it to be otherwise for us? And if Jesus spent thirty years preparing for three and a half years of ministry, we too should not be surprised if God spends a large portion of our lives building our manhood or womanhood before launching us into our ultimate ministry. To maintain our ministry and mature in it, then, we must make sure we allow God the time and process He requires to make us into the man or woman that He knows will be needed for us to be and do what He has called us to.

Judging Ministers. In judging true and false ministers, the quality of manhood or womanhood must be judged. We must evaluate ministers apart from their ministry, position, title, or gifting. In such an evaluation, we should ask ourselves, Is this the kind of person I would want for my best friend, neighbor, or co-laborer in God's kingdom throughout eternity?

I have known mighty, miracle-working ministers who had built great spiritual works—yet in their personal manhood or womanhood they had so many unChristlike attributes that I wouldn't want them as a personal friend. I wouldn't want to spend my vacation with them, much less eternity.

Remember: We may not manifest our present ministry throughout eternity, but we will be the type of person we are in eternity. I can find no scriptural text that declares we will receive a transformation of character at death or at the return of the Lord. The resurrection-translation of the saints at the end of the age is designed to change only one thing: Our physical bodies will be transformed from mortal to immortal (Phil.3:21; 1Cor.15:51; 1Thess.4:17).

On the other hand, Christlike character comes about through a different transformation—the "renewing of our minds" (Rom. 12:2), the continual change into His image from glory to glory (2Cor. 3:18). With this truth in mind, John declared:

> Beloved, now we are children of God, and it has not appeared as yet what we shall be. We know that, when He appears, we shall be like Him, because we shall see Him just as He is. **And everyone who has this hope fixed on Him purifies himself, just as He is pure** (1John 3:2,3 NASB).

These are some of the reasons God has more concern about ministers being real men and women with Christlike character than being mighty ministers.

2. MINISTRY. The second area to which we must give attention if we are to mature in ministry is the fruits of that ministry. Jesus pointed to this area when He warned His disciples about false prophets who would come to them as ferocious wolves in sheep's clothing. He said of true ministers that "by their fruit you will recognize them" (Matt.7:15-20 NIV).

How long does the positive effect of our ministry last? Is it all froth, or is there abiding fruit? After all the excitement, shouting, singing, and dancing is over, what remains that is of value?

Does our ministry manifest the anointing of God—that is, the divine enablement of grace to accomplish God's intended results? Or is there more talk than true power? The apostle Paul insisted: "My message and my preaching were not with wise and persuasive words, but with a demonstration of the Spirit's power, so that your faith might not rest on man's wisdom, but on God's power…. The kingdom of God is not a matter of talk but of power" (1Cor.2:4,5; 4:20). We have no excuse for not demonstrating the supernatural dimension of spiritual gifts in our ministry.

Is our preaching or prophesying productive? Is the word we speak positive, pure, and proven? Have we been accurate, and has our ministry produced the fruit of the Spirit in those to whom we've ministered?

Though we are no longer under the Mosaic Law, we should keep in mind the seriousness in God's eyes of ministering in His name. He told the ancient Israelites: "But a prophet who presumes to speak in my name anything I have not commanded him to say—must be put to death" (Deut.18:20 NIV).

How do we know whether our words have been truly of God? In the same biblical passage, God told the people how to judge: "If what a prophet proclaims in the name of the Lord does not take place or come true, that is a message the Lord has not spoken. That prophet has spoken presumptuously" (vv. 21,22 NIV).

In addition, we should consider whether our preaching or prophesying has caused people to stumble or has discredited the ministry in any way. Paul was able to declare: "We have put no stumbling block in anyone's path, so that our ministry may not be discredited" (2Cor.6:3 NIV). He went on to report how he and those who ministered with him had endured hardship, opposition, hard work, slander, and deprivation, yet through it all they had given no one genuine cause to condemn their work.

This is not to say, of course, that our ministry should never stir controversy or criticism; even Paul had those problems in abundance. But it is to say that we should suffer for the sake of truth and righteousness in our ministry, not for the sake of unnecessary stumbling blocks we have erected by causing undue offense (1Pet.4:15).

Function in Full Authority. I want to encourage and challenge all Christian ministers to function in their full authority as New Testament ministers. The apostle Paul said that God "hath made us able ministers of the new testament; not of the letter, but of the Spirit: for the letter killeth, but the Spirit giveth life" (2Cor.3:6). He was emphasizing the great truth that born-again, Spirit-filled ministers can minister the Holy Spirit gifts and graces as easily as they preach the Logos Word of God.

All that the Holy Spirit has been commissioned to be and do for the Church, the New Testament minister can minister to God's people. The revelation of this truth gave me the faith to minister spiritual things with the same authority and anointing I have in preaching the Word. Those ministers who understand this truth, and are ministering the Spirit the same way they minister the letter of the Word, are those I would call "prophetic ministers."

All New Testament ministers need to become able ministers in the Holy Spirit to prove that they truly manifest the kind of ministry God intends for them. In light of this application of Paul's words, all Christian ministers should be prophetic ministers, and all saints should manifest prophetic ministry.

This is one reason Paul commanded the Corinthian Christians to "desire spiritual gifts" (1Cor.14:1) and "covet to prophesy" (v.39), for we "may all prophesy (manifest prophetic ministry) one by one" (v.31). Let's all obey the admonition of Paul to make full proof of our ministry by properly ministering both the **Word and the Spirit** of God.

3. MESSAGE. The Bible says we should be "speaking the truth in love" (Eph.4:15). Paul tells us here that the message of a mature minister should first of all be life-giving present truth. It should present the Word of God in a way that is thoroughly scriptural, doctrinally sound, and well-balanced in the light of the full testimony of the Bible.

Second, Paul says, the message should be spoken in **love**. Not just the content but also the **spirit** of the message should be right. For it is possible to be doctrinally right, but spiritually wrong.

Our preaching, teaching, and prophesying can be scriptural, theologically sound, and well-balanced, yet still be delivered with a tone, a motivation, and a spirit that is out of order because it is not according to divine love. The Pharisees had some right doctrine, but their spirit, their attitude, and their relationship with God were all wrong. They were full of pride, narrow-mindedness, and self-righteousness.

Of course, the converse is true as well. We can have the right spirit, attitude, and motivation—we can be quite loving and humble—and yet have wrong doctrine. So we cannot judge the doctrinal correctness of a minister on how much we like him or her personally. We must judge sound theology solely on the Bible.

At the same time, biblical orthodoxy and supernatural **power** don't always go together. I have met many teachers and other ministers who are doctrinally correct, yet they manifest little divine anointing or power. On the other hand, we cannot judge a person's message to be doctrinally sound simply because he or she is able to perform signs and wonders. This reminder will become increasingly important in these last days as the devil manifests his supernatural power more and more through counterfeits of God's works.

Yet another truth we must keep in mind in the area of message is that God blesses His Word, and He confirms it. When the disciples went out to fulfill the Great Commission after Jesus had ascended into heaven, the Scriptures tell us: "Then the disciples went out and preached everywhere, and the Lord worked with them and **confirmed His Word** by the signs that accompanied it" (Mark 16:20 NIV).

The Bible does not say here that "God confirmed their great statements of faith lest they look like fools, lest they be embarrassed and their fleshly ego be deflated." No—God does not confirm us; He confirms His **Word**.

We must not say, "I quoted Scripture; I took a stand. Now, God, your reputation is at stake; you've got to back me up!" If we do, the Lord will answer, "Who says? I don't have to save my reputation. My reputation is not at stake; it's not based on anything anybody does. I'm God; I'm Eternal; nobody will hurt Me."

The Bible says that Jesus, who is God, did not worry about His reputation; in fact, He "made Himself of no reputation" (Phil.2:7). He didn't try to become popular or famous; He never said, "Would you make sure that miracle gets in the newspaper?" He just wanted to do the will of the Father, and the message that came out of His mouth was the Word of the Lord.

God confirms His Word; not our flesh, our desires, or our presumption. He is not concerned to preserve our fleshly pride. He is concerned that we have a good report, that we portray the gospel correctly, that we fulfill His will. But He is not concerned with our popularity. Once we realize that truth, we can release ourselves from a great deal of pressure.

Have you ever wondered why some ministers who preach the Word of God but live lives of sin have nevertheless had results? We've all read or heard about preachers or evangelists who were exposed as adulterers or alcoholics, and yet even while they sinned habitually, people were saved, healed and delivered through their preaching of God's Word.

Why, we ask, does God seem to give approval to their behavior this way? Why does He confirm the lives of such people? The answer, of course, is that He does not **confirm** them; He confirms His **Word** that they preach. An atheist could stand up in a packed stadium and read John 3:16, and some people would probably give their hearts to the Lord as a result. That's because God's Word has power in itself, and God confirms His Word. The gospel itself, not the one who preaches it, is "the power of God unto salvation" (Rom.1:16).

We should not be surprised, then, that on judgment day the Lord will be able to say that He never knew some who in His name prophesied, cast out demons and performed miracles (Matt.7:23). He will say, "Yes, you proclaimed My name, you used My gifting, and I confirmed My Word. But your life was not in line with My character; I can't take you."

All ministers and church members need to study continually the Word of God to show themselves approved to God (2Tim.2:15). Our message must be not only biblically balanced in the fundamentals of the Christian faith, but also "established in the present truth" (2Pet.1:12). For us to minister and mature in our "M" of message, we must retain the basic while continuing to incorporate all presently restored biblical truths into our message.

4. MATURITY. The Bible wisely warns us not to place new Christians in places of leadership, but to wait until they have had a chance to be proven and to mature (1Tim.3:6). Even so, maturity does not come automatically with time.

The traits of maturity in the Christian life are listed by Paul when he recites for the Galatians the fruit of the Spirit: love, joy, peace, patience, kindness, goodness, faithfulness, gentleness, and self-control (Gal.5:22,23). In addition, we can add to this list the fruit of godly wisdom, which James says is pure, peaceable, considerate, submissive, full of mercy and good fruit, impartial and sincere (James 3:17). But sadly enough, all too many ministers have failed to allow the dealings of God and hard experience to cultivate in them a divine maturity.

The truly mature person manifests the characteristics of God's **agape** love Paul described to the Corinthians: patient, kind, not envious, not boasting, not proud, not rude, not self-seeking, not easily angered; not keeping a record of wrongs; not delighting in evil but rejoicing with the truth; always protecting, trusting, hoping, persevering; never failing (1Cor.13:4-8). (For more on the proper spirit of God's true prophets, see chapter 9 of the second volume in this series.)

Have you ever tried to handle a person with extensive burns? Their injury makes it almost impossible for them to be touched without feeling pain. They are like a bundle of raw nerves, sensitive to the slightest touch.

I have known some ministers who are like that in their personality and their emotions. You have to be careful when you're around them, because the slightest negative word or glance makes them feel injured. They tend to be unapproachable, untouchable, defensive, touchy.

Such people need to grow enough emotional "skin" to recover from their injuries and to be covered properly. So essentially their problem is immaturity, and it can only be resolved by emotional and spiritual growth.

God Is Looking for Faithful Servants. Faithfulness is also an important quality of maturity. When the master in Jesus' parable commended his servant, did he say, "Well done, great spiritual prophesier, miracle worker, prophet, apostle"? No. He said, "Well done, **good** and **faithful** servant" (Matt.25:21). On the day of judgment, we will not be judged by how many books we wrote, how many people knew our name, how many countries we traveled in, how many people we ministered to, or whether or not we became a pastor or bishop. God will ask, "Were you good and faithful?"

Did you ever hear about the famous minister who stood before the Lord, and the Lord asked, "What did you accomplish for me?"

"Well, Lord," said the minister, "what do you think about those ten books I wrote?"

"I don't know," the Lord answered. "I never read them."

God is not as impressed with all our achievements as we tend to be. But He is impressed with our goodness and faithfulness.

"When I was a child," Paul writes, "I talked like a child, I thought like a child, I reasoned like a child. When I became a man, I put childish ways behind me" (1Cor.13:11 NIV). Can we say the same thing? Have we learned to put behind us the selfishness, possessiveness, and desire for attention that can only be labeled childishness, unfitting for a mature son or daughter of God?

Theological Maturity. Meanwhile, emotional and social maturity are only part of the picture. Have we also grown mature in our theology and in our understanding of Scripture? Or is our doctrine still simplistic, shallow, self-serving, or narrow-minded?

Are we still "infants, tossed back and forth by the waves, and blown here and there by every wind of teaching and by the cunning and craftiness of men in their deceitful scheming" (Eph.4:14 NIV)? Hebrews says that we must go beyond feeding on the "milk" of elementary teachings to the teaching of righteousness that is "solid food" for the mature, "who by constant use have trained themselves to distinguish good from evil" (Heb.5:12-14 NIV).

Loving Jesus Is the Key. What is a mature person? Mature people are those who have overcome their character flaws. They have been delivered from their weed-seed attitudes and they are no longer subject to the "prophet syndromes."

We will never reach our full potential unless we allow God to bring our manhood or womanhood to maturity. In many places the Bible reminds us of the necessity of continually growing until we reach full maturity. And the Bible makes it clear that the key to maturity is loving Jesus Christ with our whole being and allowing Him to be the Lord of every area of our lives.

5. MARRIAGE. Yet another critical area that deserves our attention as ministers is our marriage and family life. God's Word is clear: Our marriage is to reflect the kind of loving relationship we find between Christ and the Church (Eph.5:22-33). Wives must respect and submit to their husbands even as husbands respect and live considerately with their wives (1Peter 3:1,7). And husbands must love their wives with Christ's kind of love—not lording it over them, but treating them as fellow-heirs of the grace of God. Otherwise, our prayers—and our ministry in general—will be hindered (1Peter 3:7).

Our spouses should be our best friends. If we find that someone else is growing closer to us than our own spouse, then we are in danger of an "emotional adultery" that could lead to worse things.

Our home must be in biblical order. Our children must be well-disciplined and well-cared for (1Tim.3:2-5). But at the same time, we must not take our concern about our children's behavior to the kind of extreme that demands they provide perfect models all the time "for the sake of the ministry." This kind of unrealistic expectation can lead to our children resenting and rebelling against the local church, especially if they are also expected to make continual sacrifices "for the sake of the ministry." That is part of what Paul meant when he said: "Fathers, do not exasperate your children" (Eph.6:4 NIV).

Ministry Must Not Compete with Family. Meanwhile, we must not allow the ministry to deny us adequate time and energy to build a healthy relationship with our children, as is all too often the case with ministers. If that happens, then we're likely to learn the truth of a common formula for family disaster: Rules without relationship lead to rebellion.

This takes us to the matter of priorities. The proper order of priorities in our lives is God first, wife and children second, and ministry third. To keep this order intact, many times we must simply draw a line and decide that on a particular occasion, when ministry to others threatens to encroach on our ministry to our family, we must choose in favor of our family.

This is true even in seemingly small matters. Take the telephone, for example. When we're in the middle of dinner, a serious conversation with our spouse, or some other important family time, if the phone rings do we automatically jump up to answer it? If we do, then we may be saying to our family that the phone—and the people we minister to on the other end of the line—are more important to us than they are.

There may be times when we must choose to let the phone ring. Otherwise, we may end up spending more time fathering others than being a true husband and father to our wife and children.

I once counseled with a man whose marriage was in trouble and who came to me to say that he believed his wife was hindering his ministry. He wanted a divorce.

In his estimation, his wife didn't share his zeal and his burden for the ministry. He lamented long and loud the great needs of the Church, which he declared to be the beloved Bride of Christ. He emphasized the blessing he could be to the Church if he just didn't have the problem of his wife's being a weight of resistance, which was causing him to sin against God by not fulfilling his preaching ministry. He even felt the Holy Spirit had given him scripture to justify his plans to divorce his wife: "Lay aside every weight, and the sin which doth so easily beset us" (Heb.12:1).

I told him clearly that I believed such a divorce would be contrary to God's will, and that his marriage needed to take priority over his ministry. I urged him to go home and love his wife the way Christ loved the Church. But he didn't seem convinced by what I said, and he was apparently disappointed that I didn't agree with his reasoning.

Some time later I saw him again, and he told me that he was working out his relationship with his wife. When I asked him what had changed his mind, he told me that one day in prayer he had been crying out to the Lord, "God, your Bride is in such bad shape; she needs help! I have to be free from my wife so that I can take care of your Church!"

Then God surprised him with His reply. He said, "Do you really think I'm going to entrust my Bride to you when you can't even take care of your own bride?" As the apostle Paul posed the question to Timothy (1Tim.3:5): If we can't care for our own household, how can we care for the household of God?

6. METHODS. Hypocrisy is one of the greatest underminers of ministry. The problem of ministers whose practice doesn't match their preaching goes back to biblical times, as attested by Paul's words to Titus: "They claim to know God, but by their actions they deny him" (Titus 1:16 NIV).

We could paraphrase this passage today to say: "They profess that they're charismatic, present-truth, prophetic people. They confess that they're Christians and children of God. They claim to be God's ministers. But they deny him by their unChristian, ungodly methods."

In our ministry methods, we must be what I like to call "rigidly righteous." We must have no mercy on the works of the flesh; we must treat them like rattlesnakes, to be avoided and put to death at all costs.

In ministry as in any other endeavor, the end does not justify the means. We cannot conclude, for example, that in order to impress people more deeply with God's power and grace, we can justify exaggeration in our personal testimony or in relating some miracle we have witnessed. Maintaining proper methods precludes what I jokingly call "speaking evang-elastic-ally"— that is, stretching the truth. We must walk in absolute integrity.

I have read newspaper accounts before in which an evangelist was quoted as saying that thousands attended a meeting and hundreds came forward to the altar. Yet I was at those meetings myself, and I knew that the numbers were considerably lower. When I asked the evangelists why they didn't tell the truth, they explained: "If I give numbers that are big, more people will get excited and turn out the next night, and more will be saved. So my little lie results in more people going to heaven."

I doubt that "more souls" was the only motivation for such deception; the evangelist probably also wanted to look more successful. But even if evangelism was his only motivation, the method would still be wrong. The end does not justify the means, and a lie cannot serve the truth.

Honesty in Finances. We must also practice absolute honesty in our finances and be ethical in all our ministry dealings with others, especially in fund raising. Some ministries, for example, manufacture "crises" or use guilt manipulation to squeeze donations out of Christians. But we must be above those sorts of questionable tactics.

I read every book I could find on financial prosperity, and I must say that the faith movement has brought forth some important truths concerning biblical methods in this area. Oral Roberts' book on seed faith was a particular help to my wife in gaining the biblical concept that we must sow money to reap money. The spiritual law of sowing and reaping has certainly worked in our lives: We began applying it long ago, and by the late 1970's we were completely out of debt. Since then we have stayed out of debt and have personally continued to prosper as we give abundantly.

Sadly enough, however, some ministers have used this truth to take large "prove me offerings" for themselves. The truth they taught was right, but the minister's motives and methods were wrong. In light of that practice, I'm concerned about unscrupulous, self-promoting ministers using the truth of the "prophet's reward" and "prophetic offerings" to manipulate people selfishly. I anticipate that some prophetic ministers with the wrong motive will promise Christians in return for big offerings to their own ministries a prophet's reward. The promise of a continuing financial supply plus the miracles money can't buy are only parts of the prophet's reward. The Bible plainly speaks of a person being specially rewarded for blessing a prophet in the name of a prophet. But when Jesus made this statement He never intended it to be used as a tool for ministers to manipulate people for their own selfish purposes (Mt.10:41).

In addition, keeping our word, paying our bills, maintaining accurate records, and treating our staff members with basic kindness all come under the requirements of proper methods. Paul speaks in Romans of those "who hold the truth in unrighteousness" (Rom.1:18). Such people have the truth of God, but they are not right in their methods. According to Paul "the wrath of God is revealed" against them. If we expect to be used by God in this Prophetic movement, the Lord will not allow us to get by with anything less than "rigid righteousness."

For forty years, the Israelites wandered in the wilderness without being circumcised. But when they crossed over the Jordan River to take Canaan, God required that they cut away the flesh and consecrate themselves through circumcision (Joshua 5:1-8).

I believe that the charismatic movement has been like that wilderness wandering. Christians came out of the Egyptian bondage of dead religion, but they have in many ways only wandered in the wilderness, still carrying the flesh of ungodliness and not yet entering into God's promised land. I believe that God was gracious during that time and did not call to account many ministers who were not scrupulous in their methods.

Nevertheless, I also am convinced that the Prophetic movement is taking us over Jordan and into our Canaan to conquer it. So I believe that God will not allow us to remain uncircumcised. He will require of us that we cut away the flesh of ungodly methods and consecrate ourselves to Him in holiness. And He will call us to account if we don't.

7. MANNERS. When Paul wrote Titus, he included in his letter a list of qualifications for an overseer, as well as reminders about how all the people were to behave. These instructions help us see the kind of manners that should characterize God's ministers:

> Since an overseer is entrusted with God's work, he must be blameless—not overbearing, not quick-tempered, not given to drunkenness, not violent, not pursuing dishonest gain. Rather he must be hospitable, one who loves what is good, who is self-controlled, upright, holy and disciplined.... Remind the people to be subject to rulers and authorities, to be obedient, to be ready to do whatever is good, to slander no one, to be peaceable and considerate, and to show true humility to all men" (Titus 1:7,8; 3:1,2 NIV).

All Christians, but especially Christian ministers, should be different from the world in their manners. Love must be the rule for their relations to others—and love is not just a feeling. Love is a principle we practice, a way of life. Love is gentle, polite, kind, and discreet; self-controlled, peaceable, considerate, and slow-tempered. In short, love is mannerly; and the manners of a Christian minister should show him or her to be a gentleman or a lady.

A Poor Example. We once sent a team of several prophets overseas to bless a conference of ministers. All the prophets gave accurate prophetic words; their preaching was sound and many miracles accompanied their ministries. But the national coordinator requested that one of the visiting ministers in particular not come back to that nation.

Their complaint was not about his ministry, but his manners. He had been rude, demanding, selfish and disrespectful to most of those with whom he had come into contact, from waitresses in restaurants to the host coordinator. The host said he had to follow him making apologies for him.

Even a seemingly little "M" like manners can close doors to people and their ministries. A prophet has no excuse for being rude, crude, ill-mannered or obnoxious. On the contrary, true prophets of God will portray proper, Christlike manners in their dealings and ministry with others.

Gentlemen Aren't "Sissies." In the rural Oklahoma culture in which I was raised, the manners of a gentleman were not valued. Gentlemen were considered "sissies." I was taught as a boy to be rough, tough, and mean. So it took years of God working on me to teach me that His standard for Christian ministers was not a macho hardness, but rather a gentle kindness. I wonder how many other men might have the same kind of upbringing to have to overcome.

One requirement for ministers that is especially important here is that they "slander no one." Another translation says that we must "speak evil of no one." That means we must guard our tongues when talking about our relatives, our neighbors, our boss, our employees—even our enemies. Our speech, as Paul told the Colossians, should be always "full of grace, seasoned with salt" (Col.4:6 NIV).

No Coarse Language. Another type of speech that must be avoided is coarse language. Paul told the Ephesians: "Do not let any unwholesome talk come out of your mouths, but only what is helpful for building others up" (Eph.4:29 NIV). Profanity, vulgarity, blasphemy, and other impure language simply have no place in the vocabulary of a minister of the gospel of Jesus Christ.

Jesus said, "Out of the abundance of the heart the mouth speaketh" (Matt.12:34). If we tend to use foul language under stress, then we need to get the foulness out of our heart. We must ask God to deliver us and to set a guard over our lips.

In whatever form, ill manners will tend to discredit our ministry. Are we on time for our appointments, or do we keep people waiting? Do we write thank you notes for gifts and other kindnesses, or do we forget to show gratitude? Do we wait our turn in conversation, or do we tend to interrupt others as they speak? Do we treat store clerks with respect, or are we impatient and demanding? Even in small matters, when we deal with others we need to remember that we have no excuse for rudeness.

"Love is patient, love is kind. It does not envy, it does not boast, it is not proud. It is not rude, it is not self-seeking, it is not easily angered, it keeps no record of wrongs" (1Cor.13:4,5 NIV). Ministers of God are called to be ladies and gentlemen.

8. MONEY. Money is neither good nor evil in itself. It is an inanimate object with neither virtue nor vice. Money is simply the medium of exchange for earthly things, just as faith is the medium of exchange for heavenly things. Money is merely earth's currency for purchasing human services and material items.

The Bible teaches that the **love** of money is the root of all evil (1Tim.6:10). But the Bible doesn't teach that it's wrong to be wealthy. Some of the richest people on earth in their day were some of God's chosen people, such as Abraham, David, Solomon, and Job.

It's God's will that His people prosper and be in good health, even as their soul prospers (3John 2). God loves to give abundantly to His children, but they are not to have a love for an abundance of earthly things. He promises that if we seek first

His kingdom and His righteousness, then all the material things we need will be added to us (Matt.6:33).

The Christian can have money, but money must not have the Christian. It's a matter of heart attitude, motive, and biblically ordered priorities. The love for the earthly power that wealth can give has been for many the instrument to indulge "the lust of the flesh, the lust of the eyes, and the pride of life" (1John 2:16). Money isn't sinful, but it can certainly provide the opportunity for sinful desires to be fulfilled, just as money can provide the means for the righteous to do great things for the kingdom of God.

The Love of Money. The Bible confirms what we might conclude from some headlines in recent years: The love of money can get ministers in deep trouble. Paul wrote to Timothy:

> People who want to get rich fall into temptation and a trap and into many foolish and harmful desires that plunge men into ruin and destruction. For the love of money is a root of all kinds of evil. Some people, eager for money, have wandered from the faith and pierced themselves with many griefs" (1Tim.6:9,10 NIV).

Sadly enough, in recent times we often heard an extreme teaching that said the wealthier you were, the more material things you had, the greater proof it was that you were spiritual and had great faith. On the contrary, however, if material gain shows that a person is godly, then all the rich people of the world should be godly—and we know that is obviously not true.

I believe that if we trust and obey the Lord, He will supply all our needs and prosper us. But we can never assume that simply because we have cars and boats and houses and lands, those things are a sign of God's approval on our lives. Paul assures us that those who "suppose that gain is godliness" are mistaken. On the other hand, "godliness with contentment is great gain" (1Tim.6:5,6 NIV).

Consequently, we must realize that if we pray for wealth, we are praying for temptations, snares, and heartaches. The higher we go up the mountain of financial "success," the less the vegetation grows, the harder the wind blows, and the lonelier it is. I've seen very few ministers who became wealthy and yet were still able to maintain integrity in their other "M's."

For that reason, we should follow Paul's warning to "flee from all this, and pursue righteousness, godliness, faith, love, endurance and gentleness" (v.11 NIV). To that we can add Jesus' own words: "Watch out! Be on your guard against all kinds of greed; a man's life does not consist in the abundance of his possessions" (Luke 12:15 NIV).

Practical Guidelines. Prophetic ministers would do well to follow a few practical guidelines for their use of money. In particular, we should note that of all the "10 M's," money is probably the most sensitive area for the relationship between itinerant and local ministers. The giving and receiving of offerings and honorariums can lead to touchy issues. I have pastored locally and also traveled in ministry, so I can tell you from firsthand experience that both pastors and traveling ministers are sometimes abused and their funds misused.

At CI, we have made it a policy always to do the best we can financially for a guest speaker, but we can't speak for everyone. Local ministries range widely in their attitudes toward honorariums: Some are quite generous, others are downright dishonest, most give at an average level.

Guidelines for the Local Minister. I would offer a few simple rules for the local minister, usually a pastor, who invites a guest speaker in to speak at a church meeting or conference. First, you should have an established minimum that you give anyone who comes to minister. At the present time in the United States,

I would recommend that this minimum be between two hundred and five hundred dollars.

In twenty-five years of extensive traveling ministry, I have received anywhere from $100 to $5,000 for one service, and from $1,000 to $10,000 for a week of meetings at one church. These were special honorariums given me personally as a guest minister.

Standard practice is for the local ministry to pay for all travel expenses round trip. If guest ministers are on a long itinerary, then general policy is to pay the travel expense to bring them from where they last ministered and to take them to the next place of ministry.

In my experience, most denominational churches don't take up a special offering to give exclusively to the guest minister, especially those with larger congregations (over 500 people). Instead, they usually have a set amount for Sunday meetings and midweek services. Non-denominational churches, on the other hand, tend to take up a special offering to give exclusively to the minister.

Factors Affecting the Honorarium. A number of factors will determine whether the honorarium is minimum, average, or abundant: Did the local and translocal ministers allow God to get involved in the honorarium? Did the pastor initiate the invitation to the guest minister, or did the guest minister request opportunity to speak at the church? Is the guest minister seasoned, with years of proven ministry, or is he or she still young in the maturing process?

Perhaps most important, was the ministry to the church average, or did the guest minister give him or herself to extra hours of ministry in prophesying to individuals, praying for the sick, or being instrumental in causing many souls to be saved, bringing new families to the church, or raising money for the church? The minister who just teaches for an hour, fails to pray for anyone, and simply leaves to go eat and have fellowship should receive different consideration from one who preaches for an hour and then goes on to prophesy and minister to scores of people the gifts of the Spirit, either laying on hands individually or praying for large groups at a time.

Avoiding Discouragement. It can be quite discouraging to dedicated, anointed ministers who give themselves unselfishly to the saints for hours of heavy ministry when the pastor gives them a minimal offering. In that situation, much grace is required to keep a positive attitude and the joy of the Lord.

Let me share a vital truth and attitude that has kept my wife and me from becoming discouraged, resentful or bitter when offerings were not in proportion to ministry given or did not come close to meeting our basic needs. Itinerant ministers must take the attitude: "I'm working directly for God, and He writes my paycheck." We must always remember that God is our source, not the local pastor, the church, or anyone else.

No doubt God doesn't make money in heaven and then send it to us on earth. Money is made and distributed on earth by people. But God is the One who is faithful to lead people to give according to His promise to us.

When my wife and I took this attitude, we found that God will always find someone who is willing to respond to His direction to give above average. Their giving is then able to make up for those who did not have the heart and vision to give sufficiently to match our ministry and meet our needs.

Some Personal Examples. To give an example or two: In our early days of ministry, I ministered every night for two weeks in a particular church. My wife was in her ninth month of pregnancy with our son Tom.

Every night I preached and ministered prophetically to ten to twenty people. Though I was there fourteen days, the pastor never took up an offering for me until the last night. There were about a hundred and twenty-five people attending regularly, with many new people each night.

The pastor gave me the offering in an envelope just as I was leaving to take my wife to have our baby. When I opened the envelope, I found only eighty-five dollars in it. My heart sank.

The pastor could easily have received five times that much for me if opportunity had been given to the people more often during the two weeks of ministry. But as it was, that eighty-five dollars was all we had to our name. And I needed several hundred dollars to put my wife in the hospital for delivery.

After grumbling and complaining awhile, we remembered that God was our employer, and He would write the paycheck. When people fail, God remains faithful.

When we arrived in Yakima Valley, Washington, where our baby was to be delivered, a minister invited me to speak for three nights. The honorarium he gave me was two hundred and forty-three dollars. Another minister had me speak just on Sunday morning, but gave me seventy-five dollars. In that one service I received almost as much as I'd been given for two weeks of preaching, praying and prophesying in that other church.

God keeps the record of our labor of love. When pastors and others don't do us right, He'll cause others to provide a super-abundance. Over all these years, the economy has changed and the figures have increased about ten times. But the principle of God's faithfulness has never changed.

Not long ago, for example, we ran into a problem when we discovered that a group that had invited me to minister did not believe in women ministers. My wife nearly always travels with me in ministry as a co-speaker and prophetic minister; she and I come as a "package deal," and for years our hosts have willingly paid travel expenses for both of us. So I insisted that she be with me on this trip as well. But our hosts refused to pay for my wife's ticket, which was over six hundred dollars.

We paid for the ticket. Then, after four days of ministry at the gathering, I received only a thousand dollars. That meant the two of us only netted four hundred dollars for four days of preaching and prophesying to hundreds of people. It was the lowest offering I had received in over a decade.

Nevertheless, God is faithful. He had me speaking in a four-day conference the following week that not only paid my wife's ticket and covered all our expenses, but also gave us an offering of four thousand, five hundred dollars.

The traveling minister must realize that God works on the law of averages. He will find faithful people who will give sufficiently to meet all our needs according to His riches in glory (Phil. 4:19).

Some Unethical Practices. In our years of ministry we have also encountered some unethical practices on the part of a few local pastors. On several occasions, a pastor would use our name and ministry as the reason for taking an offering. At least several hundred dollars would be given by the people (we knew, because individuals would tell us later how much they had given)—yet as we were leaving, the pastor would give us a sealed envelope with less than a hundred dollars in it.

This practice is obviously dishonest. It's wrong for a pastor to urge his people to give, saying every penny of the offering will go to the guest minister, and then in reality give only a small portion of the offering to the guest.

The traveling ministry is one of the few professions in which you agree to render services without any idea of what the financial remuneration will be. You can see why some ministers, after being cheated a few times in this way, want to have a guarantee up front or perhaps even a contract signed before they will come to minister.

Unethical Itinerants. In a similar way, pastors can tell you about visiting ministers who have demanded the right to take their own offering. Other itinerants have been known to beg and press for funds to support an overseas orphanage, and then never send any of the offering to the institution as promised. Still others have used biblical principles of giving to prophetic ministry in order to manipulate people into giving thousands of dollars. In fact, I know of some churches that have been so stripped financially by meetings held by intinerant ministers that it took several months to recover.

Obviously, unethical practices in the "M" of money are not limited to any one group. Both local and translocal ministers have been guilty of abuses.

Ministers of every type do well to remember that God considers our handling of money a serious business. He declares in the Bible that the way we acquire and dispense money will be a determining factor in whether God releases to us our true riches of spiritual ministry (Luke 16:11). If a person uses money selfishly and unethically, God says that person will not use spiritual gifts and anointing properly.

9. MORALITY. It should go without saying that sexual immorality has no place in the life of a Christian minister, and that our firm standard must be sexual purity. But I would estimate that up to a third of the charismatic and Pentecostal ministers in our generation have fallen into sexual immorality. I myself know of about fifty such pastors. If what we have seen on television is the tip of the iceberg, can you imagine what is going on in secret?

Years ago when I was in Bible college, Stanley Frodsham, an early Pentecostal teacher, said that in the 1930s he was casting demons out of a man, and one particular demon claimed to be a prince of devils who had just received an assignment from hell. He had been given authority, he insisted, to release a new horde of demons of adultery and deception within the Church. Judging from what I've seen in the last few decades, that devil may well have been giving an accurate account of his assignment.

Honor God With Your Body. The Bible warns us against sexual impurity—all sexual activity outside the bond of marriage—in no uncertain terms:

> Do you not know that the wicked will not inherit the kingdom of God? Do not be deceived: Neither the sexually immoral nor idolaters nor adulterers nor male prostitutes nor homosexual offenders—will inherit the kingdom of God.... Flee from sexual immorality. All other sins a man commits are outside his body, but he who sins sexually sins against his own body. Do you not know that your body is a temple of the Holy Spirit, who is in you, whom you have received from God? You are not your own; you were bought with a price. Therefore honor God with your body" (1Cor.6:9,10,18-20 NIV).

Of course, sexual immorality also includes illicit sexual fantasies, pornography, and sexually arousing films or television programs. These things lead us into temptation and wear down our resistance to it. Though we sometimes desire to be tempted and tantalized by the prospect of sin, God wants us to run the other direction. So with the words of the Lord's Prayer, we must say to God, "Lead us not into temptation" (Matt.6:13).

Heart Attitudes. In fact, according to Jesus' words, sexual impurity begins before the overt action of immorality. It grows in the hidden attitudes of our heart. "You have heard it said," the Lord noted, "'Do not commit adultery.' But I tell you that anyone who looks at a woman lustfully has already committed adultery with her in his heart" (Matt.5:27,28 NIV).

We may have a wrong desire to act immorally, but not have an opportunity to fulfill that desire. Yet the act of entertaining that wrong desire is itself sinful.

Once an immoral sexual act has in fact been committed, the resulting bond, I believe, is deeper than we realize. Paul says: "Do you not know that he who unites himself with a prostitute is one with her in body? For it is said, "The two will become one flesh" (1Cor.6:16 NIV). Considering that union, I think anyone who has had an illicit sexual relationship needs to be cut free from that bond and receive inner healing. In fact, I personally believe that if a man joins himself to a prostitute, he in some sense takes on all her sins and joins them to his own.

In light of these realities, we do well to heed Paul's words to the Ephesians: "Among you there must not be even **a hint** of **sexual immorality**, or of any kind of impurity" (Eph.5:3 NIV, emphasis added). The tragic results of failure in this area are sure to shipwreck a ministry.

Male/Female Relationships in the Church. Men and women of God must develop the attitude Paul exhorted Timothy to take toward the opposite sex. He said to treat "older women as mothers and younger women as sisters, with absolute purity" (1Tim.5:2 NIV). I believe this instruction would rule out full body embraces between Christian men and women, as well as full, long kissing on the mouth. Men should give women at most the same kind of quick "hug and peck" they would give to a female relative.

No minister simply decides suddenly one day that he or she will commit adultery with a friend's spouse, a secretary, a counselee, or a worship leader. Most sexual sins start out as a seed thought or a seemingly innocent or kindly action. What starts out right can end up wrong if not properly guarded and directed.

In the parable of the sower, Jesus spoke of a man who had sown nothing but good seed in his field. Yet as it began to grow, the sower noticed that the field also contained weed seeds. When the man asked how that had come about, the answer was that an enemy had sown bad seed in the field during the night (Mt.13:24-30).

Like that sower, we may sow only the seeds of a pure attitude and proper action. But our enemies, the devil and our carnal nature, will sow weed seeds of the lust of the flesh, the lust of the eyes, and the pride of life. Then subtly one of these seeds will sprout right alongside the good seed, and suddenly a look, a touch, a complimentary word will activate a fleshly, sensual desire and suggestion.

While in seed form, the two kinds of attitude and behavior looked almost identical. But once they sprout, people who are on guard against weed seeds will immediately notice a slight difference. They will be aware that the inward feelings and reactions of their heart and soul are just a little different.

At that point, the Holy Spirit will whisper with a warning: "Beware; the weed seed sown by the enemy has just sprouted." If the person is sensitive to the Holy Spirit and has a heart to be rigidly righteous, he or she will immediately pluck up the weed by not repeating that thought or action. The old saying that "an ounce of prevention is worth a pound of cure" is certainly true in these situations.

Two Applications. I believe there are at least two applications to Jesus' comment that to lust after someone in your mind is to commit adultery in God's sight. First, Jesus was saying that if a man or woman deliberately meditates on adultery with mental images, to the extent of visualizing the action and sensing the fleshly feeling of a sexual relationship with a particular person, then even though the outward sin was not committed, yet the sin of immorality took place within the heart. It was committed through deliberate desire, daydreaming, visualization, imagination, and willful meditation.

The second application indicates that the beginning of a sin in its seed thought stage is just as serious as the full-grown plant of the act. For if the seed is not rejected, it will surely sprout. And if the seed sprouts and is allowed to grow, it will eventually come to harvest time when we reap the consequences of a sinful act.

It's not a sin to be tempted with a lustful thought. But it's wrong to meditate upon the sinful suggestion with desire and enjoyment. We can't keep birds from flying by and catching our attention. But we don't have to let them light on our heads, build a nest, lay eggs, and hatch other vultures which love rotten, stinking flesh.

Every Thought in Captivity. Paul declares that we should bring every thought and imagination of the mind into captivity to the mind of Christ—that is, to holy, virtuous biblical principles, practices and thoughts. One minister has said that when he finds his mind drifting into fleshly daydreaming, he shouts the scriptural text, "God forbid that I should glory (think, meditate) save in the cross (death to the flesh) of Jesus Christ!" (Gal.6:14).

The only offensive weapon Christians have in the armor of God described by Paul (Eph.6:13-17) is "the sword of the Spirit, which is the word of God." Jesus overcame every temptation of Satan during their encounter in the wilderness by quoting scripture. We too can find numerous scriptural texts to be used against every temptation and suggestion of Satan and the selfish flesh.

If any touch, look, or close working relationship creates sexually-inclined thoughts or feelings, then they must be crucified immediately. The scriptural admonition to "flee— youthful lusts" (2Tim.2:22) and to "abstain from all appearance of evil" (1Thes.5:22) must never be forgotten as we maintain and mature the "M" of morality. (For more on this subject, see "The Deception of Ministerial Mates" in the section "Pitfalls for Prophetic Ministers.")

10. MOTIVE: When I first went to Bible college, I had what I thought was a vision to be a missionary to India. But after I studied that country and learned how terrible were the conditions there, I lost my "vision." It turned out to be, not a true vision from God, only a romantic idea of my teenage years.

Looking back now, I realize that if I'm honest I must admit that my motives in wanting to be a missionary were not pure. I had not seen myself struggling in India with poverty, hunger, sickness, and other poor conditions. Instead I had imagined myself standing on the platform, preaching, laying hands on the sick, raising the dead, bringing thousands to the Lord. I saw myself writing back home to my family about it all, and having them say, "Look! Our boy has made it. Look at the miracles. Wow—he's somebody!"

I was motivated by what I thought was an opportunity for personal glory. How many other ministers, if they were honest, would admit that they have had to crucify that same motivation?

Jesus emphasized that the hidden motives of the heart must be recognized and purified. We won't be judged just for our actions, but for our **deeds**—which includes both our actions and our motives.

For example, Jesus said, "Be careful not to do your 'acts of righteousness' before men, to be seen by them. If you do, you will have no reward from your Father in heaven" (Matt.6:1 NIV). People look on our outward behavior, but God looks on the intentions of the heart (1Sam.16:7).

Do we minister in order to serve, or in order to be seen? Are we "addicted—to the ministry of the saints" (1Cor.16:15), or do we want to be recognized as great ministers? Are we motivated by a desire to fulfill God's will, or by some personal drive, such as a lust for power, fame, pleasure, or wealth?

In short, do we minister out of a heart full of God's love? If not, then the Scripture says that our ministry is nothing: "If I have the gift of prophecy and can fathom all mysteries and all knowledge, and if I have a faith that can move mountains, but have not love, I am nothing. If I give all I possess to the poor and surrender my body to the flames, but have not love, I gain nothing" (1Cor.13:2, 3).

Beware the Weak Link. We should emphasize that few if any ministers could make a perfect "score" with regard to all "10

M's." We all have room for growth, improvement, and correction. That's why all the NPM ministers are required to allow those to whom they minister a chance to complete a form evaluating their "10 M's." We realize that each of us has areas in which we need to grow, and that others may see such areas more clearly than we can ourselves.

Nevertheless, we should never assume that just because most of these areas in our life might be in good shape, we can therefore neglect the others. It only takes one problem area to derail a ministry.

Out on the grounds of our ministry's campus, where new construction is taking place, we have a large bulldozer sitting idle. The motor still runs well and the body is in good shape, but the caterpillar treads on it are worn out, and we've been told that the rest of the machine is not worth the cost of replacing the treads. So the failure of a single part to work properly has stopped this powerful machine from being used.

The same is true of the "10 M's." It only takes one part to break down for our entire ministry to come to a screeching halt. So we must be diligent to give our attention regularly to every one of these areas. And we should keep in mind that even an area we normally consider our greatest strength, if we leave it unguarded, can easily become a double weakness.

As the old saying goes, a chain is only as strong as its weakest link. Imagine this picture: You're hanging over a cliff of tragic disaster in your ministry. The only thing holding you safe is a chain whose ten links are these "10 M's" in your own life. If any one of those links is in danger of breaking, just how safe are you?

Don't become so proud and confident of the areas that are functioning well that you ignore the area that needs work. Decide today to begin making a regular inspection of each link—each one of the "10 M's" in your life. Strengthening each one is the best way to maintain and mature a godly character that will provide your ministry with a solid and stable foundation for growth. Those who diligently keep these "10 M's" in biblical order will maintain and mature in their personal lives and prophetic ministry.

14

PROPHETS
AND
PERSONAL PROPHECY
—A SYNOPSIS

The insights of the first two volumes provide a critical foundation for ministering prophetically. So this part of the present volume offers a brief synopsis of the major points of the earlier books. Nevertheless, if you desire to practice prophetic ministry, I strongly recommend that you read volumes 1 and 2 as well. They will give you a more complete treatment of these topics and a firm historical and biblical support for what you find here. Hundreds of scriptures are used to validate the points presented in the books, but we will only note a few of those texts in these brief summaries. The following 10 or more pages will cover a few of the key truths found within the 218 pages of *Prophets and Personal Prophecy.*

God Wants to Communicate. Today through the Bible and the Holy Spirit, God desires to walk and talk with us in an individual, personal, intimate relationship. Yet not all Christians understand how to recognize the voice of the Lord. Even when they do recognize it, many do not know how to respond to it so that it can be fulfilled.

In this way as in many other ways, no individual is self-sufficient in his or her relationship with God; we all need the rest of the Body of Christ. So God has set within the Body the ministry of the **prophet** as a special voice; He has established the gift of prophecy as His voice in the midst of the congregation; and He has sent the spirit of prophecy to give testimony of Jesus throughout the world (see Rev.19:10; 1Cor.12:28).

The coming of the Holy Spirit at Pentecost and the writing of the Bible did not eliminate the need for the prophetic voice of the Lord; in fact, it intensified that need. Peter insisted that the prophet Joel was speaking of the Church age when he proclaimed, "I will pour out my Spirit in those days, and your sons and daughters shall prophesy" (Acts 2:17). Paul emphasized that truth when he told the church at Corinth to "covet to prophesy" (1Cor.14:39; see also Eph.4:11).

God still wants the revelation of His will to be vocalized. So He has established the prophetic ministry as a voice of revelation and illumination which will reveal the mind of Christ to the human race. He also uses this ministry to give specific instructions to individuals concerning His personal will for their lives.

The ministry of the prophet is not, of course, to bring about additions or subtractions to the Bible. Any new additions accepted as infallibly inspired would be counterfeits, false documents containing delusions that lead to damnation. Instead, the prophet brings illumination and further specifics about what has already been written. And the Holy Spirit's gift of prophecy through the saints is to bring edification, exhortation, and comfort to the Church (1Cor.14:3).

The Holy Spirit whispering the thoughts of Christ within a Christian's heart is obviously God's ideal and divine order for communication. But what an individual has sensed in his or her spirit should be confirmed: God's counsel is that every word needs to be witnessed to and confirmed in the mouth of two or three witnesses (2Cor.13:1). This is a critical role that can be fulfilled by the prophetic voice.

Of course, personal prophecy must never become a substitute for the individual's responsibility and privilege of hearing the voice of God for him or herself. God is a jealous God and is not pleased when we allow anything to hinder an intimate relationship and personal communication with Heaven, even if the hindrance is from a ministry He Himself has ordained. Personal prophecy must not take the place of our duty to fast, pray, and seek God until we hear from heaven ourselves!

At the same time, many people cannot hear, or will not take the time to hear, what God wants to say to them. God is usually more anxious to talk than we are to listen, but He will not always break in on our busy schedules, trying to shout over the noise of the television or social chatter (though He may occasionally catch us while we are asleep). When this is the case, the Lord often uses the voice of the prophet to speak to individuals, congregations and nations. But His greatest desire is always for His children to take quality time to wait upon Him until our mind, emotions, and will are cleared sufficiently for Him to communicate His heart and mind to us clearly.

God's Purposes for Prophets. Prophets are special to the heart of God. They participate in all of God's plans and performances on planet earth. They are to prepare the way for the second coming of Christ by bringing revelation knowledge on the Scriptures that must be fulfilled before Christ can return. Thus the restoration of the prophet ministry and the company of the prophets is the greatest sign of the nearness of Christ's coming.

The prophets not only prepare the way of the Lord; they are also to "make ready a people for the Lord" (Luke 1:17). The Bride of Christ must be made ready for her husband, and the prophets help to make the Bride grow into purity and maturity. She cannot be fully perfected without the full restoration of the apostles and prophets (Eph.4:11,12) who, along with the evangelists, pastors, and teachers, have been given special ability from Christ to perfect, equip, and mature the saints.

Prophets help these ministries to come forth in at least two ways. First, through their prophesying they reveal to believers their part to play in the church and help them to interrelate with other believers. Second, their words have the Christ-gifted ability to impart, birth, and activate in believers the ministry God has revealed for them.

The Nature of Prophecy. Prophecy is simply God communicating His thoughts and intents to humanity. In this sense the whole Bible can rightly be called prophecy. This prophetic Word (the Scripture) is complete, perfect, and fully sufficient to bring all the revelation of God that we can comprehend and appropriate. So any true prophetic word given today must be in full agreement with both the spirit and the content of the Bible.

Two New Testament Greek words are translated by our English term "word": **Logos** and **rhema. Logos** refers to the Scriptures (2Tim.2:15). This **Logos** Word is creative, self-fulfilling, powerful, true, inerrant, infallible, complete, and life-giving. It is the consistent, absolute standard by which all other expressions, concepts, revelations, doctrines, preachings, and prophecies are measured.

On the other hand, the **rhema** might be called "a word from the Word." It is that timely, Holy Spirit-inspired word from the Logos that brings life, power, and faith to perform and fulfill it: "Faith comes by hearing, and hearing by the word (rhema) of God" (Rom.10:17). The rhema must be received with faith by the hearer for it to fulfill its mission.

When we use the term "Logos," we mean the Scriptures as a whole; when we say "rhema," we mean a specific word from the Lord that applies the Logos to us individually.

Though the Logos never changes or fails, the Bible is full of rhemas to individuals that never came to pass. Actually, however, in these cases it was not the rhema of the Lord that failed, but rather the people who heard it failed to understand, interpret, believe, obey, respond, wait upon, or act upon it according to God's will and way. This is the meaning of 1 Corinthians 13:8: "Prophecies shall fail."

A **personal prophecy** is God's revelation of His thoughts and intents to a particular person, family, or group of people. It is specific information coming from the mind of God for a specific situation, an inspired word directed to a certain audience. In a broad sense, then, a personal prophecy is a rhema. But we will normally use the term "personal prophecy" in a more narrow sense in order to distinguish between directly and indirectly communicated words from God. Divine communications which come straight to us from God we will call "rhemas," while those which come to us through another human being we will call "personal prophecies."

Five Ways in Which We Receive Prophetic Ministry. In addition to Scripture, God's prophetic word usually comes to us in one of five ways:

1. The Office of Prophet. The ministry of the prophet is not a gift of the Holy Spirit, but a gift-extension of Christ Himself as the Prophet.

The five-fold ministry of the Church (apostle, prophet, evangelist, pastor, teacher) is not an external endowment like a birthday present. Instead, it is an investment of Christ's mantle for the ministries of Jesus—a divine impartation of Christ's own nature, wisdom, and power for each particular kind of performance—whether apostle, prophet, pastor, teacher or evangelist. All five, when moving in full maturity, represent Christ's full ministry to the Church. These ministries are not just an extension of Body ministry, but an extension of the headship of Christ to His Body, the Church.

The office of the prophet is designed and endowed to function in a higher realm of ministry than the Holy Spirit's gift of prophecy. This gift of prophecy operates within the saints or a minister for the general upbuilding, encouraging, and comforting of the Church (1Cor.12:10; 14:3,4). But the office of prophet is authorized and anointed to flow in the areas of guidance, instruction, rebuke, judgment, and revelation—whatever Christ chooses to speak for the purifying and perfecting of His Church.

The prophets are especially anointed to perceive what is next on God's agenda for restoration. Then they lift their voices like trumpets to alert, enlighten, and charge the Church to conquer that part of the truth to be restored at that time. The prophets are thus the eyes of the Body of Christ, the trumpeters in the army of the Lord to give a clear sound revealing the desires of the Commander-in-Chief.

2. Prophetic Preaching. Prophetic preaching is not the same as simply getting the mind of the Lord about which sermon to preach on Sunday morning, or being anointed to preach a specially-prepared message from the Bible. It is a different realm altogether. Prophetic preaching from biblical truths is the direct voice of God with the pure mind of Christ, so that even the speaker's precise words and illustrations are exactly what God wants to say to the people present in that place at that time. Though the minister does not preface his or her statements with "Thus saith the Lord," the words are just as inspired and anointed as if a prophet were to speak using that phrase. Prophetic preaching is "the oracle of God" (1Pet.4:11).

3. The Prophetic Presbytery. A third means for receiving prophetic ministry is the laying on of hands with prophecy by men and women of God who meet the qualifications of a presbyter (1Tim.4:14; Heb.6:1-2; Acts13:1-3). The presbytery serves several functions in this regard, each one calling for a different set of qualifications both in the presbyters and in the candidates. This biblical practice ministers **prophetic revelation and confirmation** of those called to leadership ministry in the church; **ordination** to the five-fold ministry; **confirmation** and **activation** of membership ministries in the Body of Christ; and **progress** in Christian maturity.

4. The Gift of Prophecy. Prophecy is one of the nine manifestations of the Holy Spirit (described in 1Cor.12) given, not on the basis of Christian maturity, but because Christ wants to bless His Church through them. So these gifts are received and administered by grace and faith (Rom. 12:6).

Prophecy is important to the life of the church because prophecy is the most edifying gift for a congregation. The other eight are focused "rifle" gifts, which normally bless one specific person or perhaps a few; prophecy is a "shotgun" gift that can bless hundreds of people at once. This is one reason why the apostle Paul told the Corinthians to covet to prophesy (1Cor.14:1,39).

5. The Spirit of Prophecy and Prophetic Song. The spirit of prophecy is the testimony of Jesus (Rev.19:10). This is not a gift or office, but an anointing arising from Christ within the believer. It takes place on occasions of special anointing in a service, or when Christians exercise their faith to be a voice through which Christ can testify. **The song of the Lord** (Col.3:16) is the spirit of prophecy expressing the thoughts and desires of Christ in song.

Putting Personal Prophecy in Perspective. Is it scriptural for an individual Christian to go to a prophet and expect to receive a specific prophetic word of direction, instruction, or confirmation? The answer is yes. The Bible provides numerous examples of peoplé, especially those in leadership, going to a prophet and asking for a "thus saith the Lord" about a particular situation. (For examples, see chapter 7 of volume 1 in this series.)

God approves of this practice as long as we do not allow personal prophecy to become a substitute for our seeking God ourselves through prayer, fasting, and searching the Scriptures. The prophet and personal prophecy are not to take the place of the inner voice of the Holy Spirit. At the same time, I have found that God will not answer questions prophetically that can be resolved by diligently seeking the Scripture. Nor will the Christ within the prophet respond positively when insincere requests are made or foolish questions are asked.

You should not go to a prophet until you are sure the Lord holds first place in your life. You should seek Him on your own first. Then you will be spiritually prepared to respond properly and more likely to hear a confirmation of what has already been birthed in your spirit.

Discovering God's Word, Will, and Way. Though personal prophecy can play an important role in helping Christians make decisions, it is by no means the only way the Holy Spirit uses to reveal God's will and way. Probably ninety percent of my decisions, major and minor, have been made without personal prophecy being the dominating or even motivating factor. But I have striven to make one hundred percent of all my decisions based upon God's Word, will, and way.

The most accurate method of making sure you do everything in harmony with Heaven is to follow these "three W's" of decision making. Determine God's **Word** on a matter, His specific **will** about it, and His **way** to fulfill it. These are like three traffic lights that must all be "green" before we can proceed on our way.

God's Word. To determine whether or not the Word gives a "green" light, expose every thought, impression, and suggestion that comes to you from any source—regardless of how spiritual or religious it may sound—to the whole Bible. To avoid entering into deception, keep a love for the truth as it is, not as you selfishly want to interpret it to be (see Zech.8:19).

Thoughts and desires should not become prayer petitions until they receive a "green" light from the Word. If your thought or desire is unscriptural, improper, illegal, or immoral according to divine principles, then you are wasting your time asking God to let you do it.

God's Will. Just as God has a general will for all humankind, He has a specific will for individuals. The Bible gives the general criteria for making many decisions in business, travel, ministry, and use of our finances. But it does not provide many specifics.

So how do we come to know the specific will of God for our lives? The Scriptures gives examples of many ways in which He can guide us specifically: divinely directed desire; a rhema or an illumination of a particular scriptural text; the prophet and personal prophecy; the gifts of the Holy Spirit; the fruit of the Holy Spirit; the witness, clearance, or restraint of the Holy Spirit; wise counsel; and confirmation from other "witnesses."

God's Way. The way of God includes His timing, methods, and necessary means to do it; the who, what, when, where, and how (but not necessarily the why); the continued guidance and control of circumstances by God; and the patience to press on until His plan is accomplished. Often God's Word and will are much easier to determine than His way. The Word can be determined by examining a Book, the will by inward personal principles and confirmations from others. But the way is a time process that must be walked out day by day, because all the details of it are rarely ever revealed ahead of time.

Prophetic Terminology. The longer we know God and the more intimately acquainted we become with Him, the better we are able to understand His words to us and so respond to them appropriately. Understanding God's words to us is not as easy as it may first seem. The Scriptures tell us that He thinks and expresses Himself according to a perspective that is much different from our own. So we must get to know God's prophetic terminology.

We believe that the Holy Spirit inspired and directed the writing of the Bible from the mind of God. So we should not be surprised to find that the Bible reveals to us something of the way God thinks. It shows us how He talks and the human terms He uses to express Himself. In particular, we can look to the books of the prophets to find God's terminology, where there are so many quotes preceded by "Thus saith the Lord."

In addition, all that Jesus said demonstrated God's way of talking. So by reading the Gospels as well as the prophets, and paying close attention to the words of Jesus there, we can gain a better understanding of the way God talks—which is what we call prophetic terminology.

Time. God's time terminology differs considerably from our own. Though He never seems to be in a hurry, He is always on time. But He often seems to take longer than we think He should. So some of the greatest failures of the greatest figures in the Bible resulted from their impatience with God as they waited for a prophecy to be fulfilled (such as Abraham's siring of Ishmael).

Judging from scriptural examples, "now" or "this day" does not necessarily mean "immediately" or "within twenty-four hours" (see, for example, 1Sam.13:1-14; 15:28). "Soon" or "quickly" can mean up to two thousand years if we take as a precedent Jesus' promise in Revelation 22:20 about the timing of His return.

Process. Whenever God promises you prophetically that certain good fruit will appear in your life, you can expect that implicit in those words is the necessary process for cultivating such fruit. If He says you will have great patience, you can look for tribulation to grow that patience. If He says you will have great faith, remember that the soil of the fruit of faith is life on the brink of disaster in need of a miracle. If God announces plans to grow, build or expand, He will first have to tear down the old building and dig up the old foundation.

I Will, You Will, We Will. When God says "I will" about great things He plans to do, He does not mean He will necessarily act by Himself apart from our involvement. Judging from His "I will" pronouncements to Moses (Ex.6:6-8), when He says "I will" He means "we will"—that is, "I will do it in you and through you; I will enable you to do it."

The Nature of Personal Prophecy. We must remember that personal prophecy will always be **partial, progressive,** and **conditional.**

First, any given personal prophecy is just a small insight into God's will for our lives. Understanding this reality should keep us from despairing when a prophecy fails to mention some area of special concern. It should also keep us from presuming that God's silence about a particular matter implies His approval.

Second, prophecy unfolds and expands gradually over the years, with each prophetic word adding new information and revelation.

Third, personal prophecies are not always fulfilled because they are conditional, whether or not any conditions are made explicit. Their fulfillment is dependent on human behavior. We can see this reality in the biblical account of God's promises to the Israelites in the wilderness (Ex.6:6-8). Though His promises included no unconditional wording, they were fulfilled for only two men out of the six hundred thousand who received them. These prophecies were cancelled by the disobedience of the others.

Responding Properly to Personal Prophecy. The biblical attitude toward prophecy is thoroughly positive; it is in fact the only ministry that the Scriptures tell Christians to covet (1Cor. 12:39, 14:1,39). To maintain the proper positive response to prophecy you receive, you should keep in mind a few guidelines:

1. Judge a **prophecy** by considering the content of the words spoken to determine whether they are true or false. Judge a **prophet** as a person by the quality of his or her life to discover whether that person is a true or false prophet. (See "The 10 M's," for criteria to use in judging a prophetic minister.) An inaccurate word from a prophet does not prove that person to be a

false prophet; all human beings are fallible, and the inaccuracy may simply have been the result of immaturity, ignorance, or presumption.

2. Record, read, and meditate on your personal prophecies. If at all possible, proper preparation should be made for an audio recording of all prophecies given. This keeps the prophetic minister accountable for what is spoken and protects him or her in case the person receiving the word should misapply, twist, or misinterpret what is heard.

3. **Prove** prophecy by biblical principles and the proper criteria for judging prophetic words, but **witness** to prophecy with your spirit. When God's Spirit is bearing witness with our spirit that a prophetic word is right, is of God, and is according to His divine will and purpose, then our spirit reacts with the fruit of the Holy Spirit: love, joy, peace, and the others.

4. Don't do what you don't witness to. If the prophecy is of God, it will come to pass.

5. War a good war with your prophecy (1Tim.1:18). When we believe God's word given us in prophecy, it gives us power to persevere through trial and adversity.

6. Do nothing differently unless the prophetic word definitely directs you to do so. Unless God gives you explicit instructions to act upon, simply continue what you were doing before you received the word; don't try to make it come to pass. On the other hand, take action immediately if you are given specific directions to do so.

7. The same attitudes we need for responding to God's Word in Scripture should be maintained as we respond to prophetic words: faith, obedience, patience, humility, meekness, and submission to the lordship of Christ.

Hindrances to the Fulfillment of Personal Prophecy. Basically, the same things that hinder us from appropriating the biblical promises also hinder us from appropriating and fulfilling our personal prophetic promises from the Lord: unbelief, pride, impatience, self-deception, negligence, procrastination, slothfulness. We may be hindered by false preconceptions about life, ourselves, and God, or by what I call "soul blockage" —that is, an emotion, willful desire, or personal ambition that gets in the way of receiving God's word. We may misapply or misinterpret a prophecy, or allow disappointment or disillusionment to hinder a word's fulfillment. Or we may be wrongly motivated by fear of man, or fail to take responsibility for the results of our own behavior. (Volume 1 of this series contains numerous biblical and contemporary examples of how these prophetic principles have worked in individual lives.)

Prophetic Training a Priority. From this brief synopsis of the insights presented in the first volume of this series, *Prophets and Personal Prophecy*, we can see that churches should make it a priority in these days to equip the saints for handling the prophetic word. This reality becomes even more clear as we go on now to review the primary points presented in the second volume, *Prophets and the Prophetic Movement*. We will only use approximately five pages to highlight a few of the vital truths found within the 238 pages of volume 2.

15

PROPHETS
AND THE
PROPHETIC MOVEMENT
—A SYNOPSIS

A Tidal Wave Coming. Today we are seeing the growth of a major restorational movement throughout the Church: the Prophetic Movement. This movement is not an end in itself, but rather a means to an end. It is a Holy Spirit inspired restorational movement predestined by God for the fulfilling of His ultimate purpose for His Church and for planet earth. Yet another movement will come to restore the office of the apostle to full position and power in the corporate Body of Christ. Then will come still another movement after that, and finally will appear the mightiest restoration movement ever to take place in history.

This final movement will be greater than the accumulation of all the restoration movements over the last five hundred years combined. It will bring about the fulfillment of all prophecies that have been spoken by all God's prophets since the world began. The final movement will not only bring Christ's Church to her full maturity and stature as His Bride; it will also continue to sweep across the nations of the world like a giant, thousand-foot tidal wave. The end result will be the literal return of Jesus Christ to set up His kingdom on earth.

The Nature of a Restorational Movement. To restore means to reactivate and reestablish something back to its original purpose and intent. Thus a restorational movement is a time when the Holy Spirit acts sovereignly within the Church to restore a biblical truth or ministry back to its proper order and function.

The Prophetic Movement, designed to restore God's ascension gift of prophet back to the Church, is the most recent of a number of movements that have appeared over the last five hundred years. These movements, their approximate dates of beginning, and the major truth each one restored are summarized in the following table:

YEAR—RESTORATION MOVEMENT—MAJOR TRUTH RESTORED

1500 - Protestant	-Salvation by grace through faith
1600 - Evangelical	-Water baptism, separation of Church and state
1700 - Holiness	-Sanctification, Church set apart from the world
1800 - Faith Healing	-Divine healing for the physical body
1900 - Pentecostal	-Holy Spirit baptism and speaking in tongues
1950 - Latter Rain	-Prophetic presbytery, praise and worship
1960 - Charismatic	-Renewal of all restored truth
1970 - Faith	-Faith confessions, prosperity
1980 - Prophetic	-Prophets and the gifts of the Holy Spirit

The Nature of a True Restoration Movement. When God gets ready to do something new, He makes preparation in certain areas. He prepares a people, a product, and a place to perpetuate His plan. The Lord Jesus then raises up a man or woman with a message and a ministry which produces a movement that further fulfills His will by various methods and means.

All of the movements listed in the previous table manifest the following seven characteristics of a true restorational move of God:

1. Divine enlightenment of certain scripture texts and revelation knowledge of truths and practices that have not been properly understood and practiced since the early days of the Church.

2. The transformation of a truth, scriptural experience or ministry from being an occasional happening for a few

into a consistent practice of thousands who participate in the movement.

3. A new anointing and authority for establishing the restored truth.

4. A small beginning in an insignificant place.

5. The power to reproduce the ministry of the restored truth by teaching, training, and activating the saints.

6. Spread of the movement's restored truths and practices, accompanied by publicity, until those truths and practices are contested by critics and controversy.

7. New songs, choruses, and other music portraying the restoration message.

A Cry for Balance, Structure, and Order. When truth is in the process of being restored to the Church, it usually swings extremely to the right, then to the left, and finally hangs straight with a balanced message, like the pendulum of a grandfather clock, in the middle of the two extremes. Those who get stuck out on the extreme left become cultic in their doctrines and practices. Those who don't make it back from the extreme right become an exclusive group who separate themselves from the rest of the Body of Christ. Then there is the group who brings itself together from both extremes to maintain a balance in proper biblical doctrine and practice as God originally intended it to be restored to the Church.

Sad to say, the "balanced" group has its problems as well. It may become so protective of the truth and so reactionary toward the extremists that they keep the original form yet lose the flow of the Holy Spirit. They may keep the purity of the doctrine yet lose the fresh anointing that restored those truths. In fact, historically, this balanced group usually becomes the main persecutors of the next restorational move of the Holy Spirit. For that reason, we must keep our wineskins flexible so that we can go from movement to movement of the Holy Spirit, incorporating into our personal lives and our churches all that God wants to restore to His Church (2Cor.3:18).

Abuses and Extremes. Like every restorational move before it, the Prophetic Movement will have its share of errors as people try to carry its truths too far or misapply them. We must try especially to avoid the following abuses and extremes:

1. An overemphasis on personal prophecy.

2. Ministering out from under the authority of church leadership.

3. Using prophecy to justify rebellion and other sin.

4. Controlling or manipulating others through prophetic ministry.

5. Using the prophetic gifting for personal gain.

6. Trying to fulfill personal prophecy out of proper timing.

7. Presumptuous, critical, and judgmental prophesying.

According to 1 Corinthians 11:19, "there must also be heresies among you, that they who are approved may be made manifest among you." There must be false prophets, the ignorant, the immature, and the wrongly motivated prophetic ministers who are improperly using the office of prophet and the ministry of prophesying, so that those who are true and proper may be made manifest. But the ideal to which we will hold is to keep proper structure, order, and practice within the movement so that nothing will be done to bring reproach upon the ministry.

The Spirit of True Prophetic Ministers. Being a true prophetic minister entails much more than speaking a true word or having a miracle ministry. Such a person must be motivated by a spirit of wisdom and love, because without these, revelation becomes radical and self-exalting. In addition, true prophets are not secluded from the people who need their ministry. They are known for their mercy, even as they execute God's Word, and they are powerful intercessors.

The Prophetic Movement vs. the New Age Movement. For every divine reality there is a demonic counterfeit, and that includes prophetic ministry. Just as the early Pentecostals were accused of speaking in tongues through demonic activity, so also prophetic ministers are now being accused of New Age practices because some of their ministry appears similar on the surface.

Nevertheless, these are only superficial similarities. The source of a supernatural phenomenon is what determines its legitimacy. Is it from the Spirit of God or from Satan? From the Spirit of truth or the spirit of error?

God utterly hates the false supernatural practices of the New Age movement. In the days to come, there will not only be battles fought against these demonic strongholds through intercessory prayer, warfare praise, and prophetic prayer and praise; there will also be public confrontations between New Age leaders and God's true prophets. The prophets are now arising, and they will continue to increase in God's purity and power until all false communication channels of the New Age, satanism and witchcraft are exposed for the wicked system that they are.

The Five-fold Ministry. Jesus gave the five-fold ministry to minister to the saints for their equipping and maturing so that they can enter into the work of their membership ministry in the living, corporate Body of Christ. With regard to these ministries, we must keep in mind five important insights:

1. All five-fold ministries are headship ministry; that is, they are an extension of Jesus Christ, the Head of the Church.

2. All five are called to govern, guide, gather, ground, and guard God's people; but each has been given special grace and gifted ability in one of these areas more than the others.

3. It is unscriptural and unwise to place any of these ministries into a box of limited anointings and activities.

4. It is detrimental to the function of the five-fold ministries to categorize them with details concerning personalities, performances, and positions.

5. Each five-fold minister knows best his or her own calling and ministry.

Preparing the Way. The Prophetic Movement has a greater potential for good or evil than any of the previous movements of church history. The coming forth of the company of prophets is the most ominous sign to the devil that his eternal doom is at hand. For the prophets are preparing the way and making ready a people for the soon return of Jesus Christ.

16

PROPHETIC PRINCIPLES TO PRACTICE

Like any genuine move of God, the Prophetic Movement emerging in the Church today is generating considerable controversy. Christians are arguing over what the Bible does and does not say, and what experience has or has not proven, about prophets and prophecy. In the course of such debate, a number of questions have been raised about the origin, nature, role and scope of prophetic ministry. Though in some cases people are merely curious, in others practical advice is needed by those who are being trained to minister prophetically.

In the first two volumes of this series, some of the more important issues have been addressed from the standpoint of those who receive a personal prophecy. But because this volume is especially for prophetic ministers and for those who are participating in and being exposed to prophetic ministry, I will present in this section a concise response to the questions that are most common from the standpoint of the person prophesying. For clarity's sake, I have arranged the material in a question-and-answer format.

Scripture and Experience. The answers here are based both on Scripture and experience. As in most areas of the Christian life, I have found these two sources of understanding to be mutually illuminating: Just as we turn to the Bible to make sense of our experience, so also sometimes our experience deepens our understanding of a scriptural text in a new way.

For example, as a youth I read the scriptural texts about being born again, but it was not until I personally received the experience of being born again that I understood those words with experiential reality. The same was true of other scriptural truths, such as baptism in the Holy Spirit, divine physical healing and deliverance from various mental and emotional problems.

The principle is especially true in my life with regard to all the realms of prophetic ministry. Nearly forty years of prophetic ministry to thousands of people and in a variety of circumstances have helped me anticipate the kinds of questions most commonly asked and provide answers that are not just theoretical, but personally proven and practical.

Of course, none of the following insights are presented as the "final word" on the issues. If there is one thing I have learned in all those years of prophetic ministry, it is that God continually does new things and is infinitely creative. Though we can always depend on His character to remain faithful and unchanging, still He often surprises us by acting in ways that do not fit our accustomed mind-sets or theological assumptions.

God is much bigger than our puny notions of Him, and the ways He speaks to human beings are richer and more varied than we could ever imagine. So we expect never to stop learning in these areas. Meanwhile, I trust the following questions and answers will provide useful insights for the prophetic minister who desires to grow.

1. IS THE OLD TESTAMENT STANDARD FOR DETERMINING A FALSE PROPHET VALID FOR NEW TESTAMENT PROPHETS AND PROPHETIC MINISTRY?

In the Old Testament, one sin cast Adam and Eve out of the garden of Eden; one mistake kept Moses out of Canaan; one sin cast Lucifer out of heaven; and one mistake caused a person to be judged a false prophet, according to the standard of the law:

> But the prophet, who shall presume to speak a word in my name, which I have not commanded him to speak, or who shall speak in the name of other gods, even that prophet shall die....When a prophet speaketh in the name of the Lord, if the thing follow not, nor come to pass, that is the thing which the Lord hath not spoken, but the prophet hath spoken it presumptuously; thou shalt not be afraid of him (Deut.18:20,22; see also Deut.13:33).

Why was the standard so strict and the punishment so harsh? Under the Mosaic law, while priests functioned as representatives of humankind to God through sacrifices and ministrations, the prophets represented God to humankind with their divine judgments and decrees, prefaced with "Thus saith the Lord." There seems to be a greater judgment for misrepresenting God to the people than for misrepresenting the people to God.

For that reason, the Old Testament prophets were required to speak the very word of the Lord each time they opened their mouths. They could not afford to speak falsely or presumptuously without the risk of leading the entire nation into error.

In addition, God highly resents anyone saying that He is the One speaking when He is not in fact involved in what is being said. It is no light thing to say, "Thus saith the Lord," or "The Lord told me" to say this or do that. The Lord pronounces judgment on those who add to or subtract from what He actually wants said in a prophecy (see Deut.13:1-11; Rev.22:18,19).

New Testament Grace. Under the grace of the New Testament, Jesus Christ is our mediator—not the prophet nor the pastor—and we have the completed canon of Scripture to rely on. This does not do away with the need for prophets and prophecy, but it does place such ministries in a less responsible position than their Old Testament counterparts. God is eternal and never changes, yet He does work with humankind according to different standards established during each dispensation. Prophets ministering in the dispensation of the Church are extended more grace than were the prophets of the Old Testament.

Consequently, the ministry of a prophet and the accuracy of his or her words provide only some of the criteria for discerning whether that prophet is true or false. More credence should be given to other areas of a prophet's personal life, such as morality, marriage, money, motive, and the other "M's" we discussed in an earlier section of this book. Keep in mind that in the section on prophetic pitfalls we presented the example of Balaam, whose words were accurate and yet who was judged a false prophet because of his character and lifestyle.

A Difficult Dilemma and Double Standard. Those who operate in the prophetic ministry are often placed in a precarious position that presents a difficult dilemma. If they present themselves as infallible and contend that their prophetic pronouncements never miss, they are deemed heretics because the Bible clearly teaches that God alone is infallible. Every fallen human being is an earthen vessel and only "sees through a glass darkly," as Paul said (2Cor.4:7; 1Cor.13:12). So we are all susceptible to error and mistakes.

Nevertheless, if prophets today should prove their fallibility by making a mistake in speaking a word that does not come to pass, then they stand accused by certain segments of the Church of being "false prophets." A few individuals, in fact, seem all too anxious for the chance to apply that label. Perhaps this dilemma is one way God has provided to ensure that His prophets will not become puffed up with pride because of their gifting or revelation. Prophets must recognize that whenever they minister they are only a "heartbeat from humiliation," so they must remain totally reliant on the grace of God for every prophetic word.

All Ministries Are Accountable. In discussing false or inaccurate prophecies, undue emphasis is often placed on the standards for prophets without considering the need for accountability among the rest of the five-fold ministries. Are any of the other ministries held to a requirement of one hundred percent accuracy in all their pronouncements? No doubt "Thus saith the Lord" demands a greater accountability because of the authority claimed in the utterance. But this does not do away with the need for accountability in a teacher's doctrine or a pastor's counsel. The apostle James notes particularly that teachers will be held to a higher standard of accountability (James 3:1).

All too often we employ a double standard. If a healing evangelist prays for a hundred sick and dying people, and two are miraculously healed, everyone is excited and shares the report of the two without mention of the ninety-eight who walked away as sick as they came. On the other hand, if a prophet ministers to a hundred people, and ninety-eight of them receive a specific, accurate word, you can be sure that folks will tend to remember the two prophecies that were inaccurate.

In trying to hold prophetic ministries accountable, some Christians develop a "witch hunt" mentality against prophets in general, seeking to discover every error made by a particular prophet. This is not the biblical pattern for accountability and will only place the investigators themselves in jeopardy of having every single one of their own sins and failures exposed for the world to see: "For in the same way you judge others, you too will be judged, and with the measure you use, it will be measured to you" (Matt.7:2 NIV). Consequently, all ministries should have a gracious attitude toward mistakes made by others, knowing that they themselves have made mistakes and will probably make many more.

A Definition of Terms. To clarify our understanding of false and inaccurate prophecies, we need to define our terms. "**False**" is defined as something not true, incorrect, wrong, untruthful, lying, unfaithful, misleading, not real. It comes from a Latin root that means "to deceive"—which implies a wrong motive, an intent to mislead.

On the other hand, "**inaccurate**" is defined simply as not accurate, not exact or correct, not according to truth, erroneous. To say a word is inaccurate implies nothing about the motive or intent of the person speaking. It only says that the word does not line up with facts as objectively considered.

Admittedly, there is some overlap in these two definitions; in common contemporary usage, the word "false" is often applied to an incorrect statement without regard to motive. Yet I believe we do well to keep these two labels distinct in order to emphasize the difference between outward factuality and inward motive, between the content of a prophecy and the character of the person prophesying.

For that reason, I reserve the term "**false prophecy**" for words spoken with wrong motives and intent, and "**false prophet**" for a prophet whose character is wrong. "False" carries the connotations of deceit, lying and wrong motives. When a minister is labeled "false," the term calls into question his or her lifestyle, doctrine, integrity and spirit.

On the other hand, I use the word "**inaccurate**" to describe a prophetic word that does not fit the established facts. To say a particular prophetic utterance is inaccurate only calls into question the specific correctness of the word spoken, not the character of the minister.

Seemingly Inaccurate Prophecies. In dealing with inaccurate prophecies, it is extremely important to substantiate a prophetic word's inaccuracy before making the judgment that it is truly wrong. Many prophecies may seem to be inaccurate at the time they are given, yet they prove to be true from the perspective of sufficient time and experience. Several biblical examples illustrate this reality.

Perhaps the clearest case of this kind of prophecy in the New Testament is Jesus' prophecy about Lazarus (John 11:4), who died of an illness. (Remember—the definition of prophecy is "God talking," so this statement qualifies.) Jesus said to His disciples: "This sickness is not unto death, but for the glory of God, that the Son of God might be glorified by it." The New International Version translates more correctly, "This sickness will not end in death."

This was an accurate prophecy—Lazarus' sickness did not end in death, because in the end, he was alive after Jesus raised him from the grave. But the disciples failed to understand what Jesus was saying at the time the prophecy was given, as well as later when Jesus said, "Our friend Lazarus sleepeth" (v. 11). So the Lord finally had to tell the disciples plainly, "Lazarus is dead" (v. 14).

Imagine what the disciples were thinking when they discovered that Lazarus was dead. They could easily have accused Jesus of giving an inaccurate prophecy, insisting, "You said the sickness wouldn't end in death, yet Lazarus has in fact died." Only several days later, when they witnessed the raising of Lazarus, were they truly in a position to judge whether Jesus' prophetic utterance had indeed been accurate.

Sometimes We Must Wait to Understand. This illustration should teach us that we do not always understand immediately the true meaning of a particular term within a given prophetic utterance. Though we can learn to interpret common prophetic terminology (for more on this topic see chapter 11 of the first volume in this series, *Prophets and Personal Prophecy*), still

God may use a word or phrase with an intention other than what we might normally expect. So we often have to wait and let time and experience prove or disprove a word.

In this case, for example, Jesus' statement that Lazarus' sickness would not "end in death" did not mean that Lazarus would not die at all. The disciples only assumed that was the meaning because up until then their experience had not normally included the raising of a dead man. Once they had sufficient experience, they could judge the accuracy of the word.

I have heard similar prophecies about finances, marriages, pregnancies and healings that sounded on the surface to be saying that everything would work out all right. Yet as it turned out, bankruptcy, divorce, miscarriage, or a worsening of physical symptoms took place before everything finally turned out all right.

Isaiah's Word to Hezekiah. A second biblical example of this type comes from the Old Testament. When King Hezekiah of Judah lay seriously ill, the word of the Lord came to the prophet Isaiah that he should tell the king: "Thou shalt die, and not live" (Is.38:1). Yet after Hezekiah begged God for an extension of his life, the Lord sent Isaiah to him again to say, "I will add unto thy days fifteen years" (v. 5). This second word was emphatic, accompanied by the miraculous sign of the sun's reversal in its path across the sky a full ten degrees.

Now imagine yourself in the place of those who might have heard the first prophecy but were not around to hear the second. When Hezekiah went on to survive another fifteen years, you most likely would have judged Isaiah's first prophecy to the king as an inaccurate one. Only if you had the further experience of being present for the second prophetic word would you have been in a position to judge the first word fairly.

A prophecy delivered in circumstances like these, if given in a public setting or shared extensively "through the grapevine," can cause many to stumble should they assume that they have all the knowledge required to make a fair judgment of its accuracy. Many times the correctness of a prophetic word can only be determined by those who know the situation well and what took place in the days that followed.

Jonah's Conditional Word of Judgment. A similar example comes from Jonah's pronouncement of divine judgment on the city of Ninevah. The word was truly from God, and it contained no conditions. It did not say, "If you repent, you will not be destroyed"; it said simply, "In forty days, Ninevah will be destroyed." Yet when Ninevah repented and sought God for mercy, God stayed the city's judgment, causing Jonah to worry about his reputation. And no wonder he worried—to many observers, it must have looked as if Jonah had prophesied inaccurately.

The truth of the matter, however, was that the prophecy was indeed a true one that nevertheless failed to come to pass because of the unspoken conditions in it arising from God's mercy. Only those who knew the whole story could judge the word fairly.

We must be careful today as well not to judge a word as not having come from God simply because an unconditional prediction never came to pass. The human response to a word can confirm or cancel it even when no conditions are explicitly noted.

A Recent Example. One of our staff members once prophesied to a woman about a nest egg of money she had, saying that God would give her wisdom in how to invest it. The woman's pastor thought the word was wrong because he knew her financial circumstances well, and she was only living from paycheck to paycheck.

Nevertheless, when he checked with her about the matter after the prophecy was given, he discovered that he had not known all the necessary facts for making that judgment. In reality, she had just received an unexpected insurance settlement that was quite substantial. The word applied to her situation perfectly.

Many prophecies are given in similar situations. So we must not be too quick to judge a word as inaccurate by the information we have. Time and experience may prove us wrong and the prophecy right.

Seemingly Inaccurate Prophecies. Even in the Old Testament, with its strict standards for prophetic accuracy, we find that a prophet of national stature once gave wrong direction to a king—yet without being labeled a false prophet or stoned for his mistake. This situation occurred when King David told his court prophet, Nathan, that he wanted to build a temple for the ark of the covenant (1Chr.17:1-4).

Nathan replied: "Do all that is in thine heart, for God is with thee." Yet that very same night, the word of God came to the prophet, correcting him and commanding him to go tell David, "Thus saith the Lord, Thou shalt not build me an house to dwell in."

A Presumptuous Word. Admittedly, the first word Nathan gave the king was not preceded by the phrase "Thus saith the Lord." Even so, the prophet nevertheless attributed the directive to God, and the biblical text seems to emphasize that the king was speaking to Nathan **the prophet.** When Nathan spoke to David, he spoke authoritatively from his position as prophet, just as David spoke to Nathan from his position as king. So we might call this a presumptuous word given out of Nathan's own spirit rather than from the Holy Spirit.

Nathan's second word to David clearly contradicted the first, showing that the first word was wrong and should therefore be disregarded. But the Bible does not mention that Nathan apologized or in any way acknowledged to David and the leadership of Israel that his initial word was in error. Evidently such a response was not necessary, and as far as the Bible tells us, the incident did not damage Nathan's reputation as a prophet of God.

That this was the case was made evident later on when Nathan confronted David with his sins of adultery and murder because of his lust for Bathsheba (see 2Sam.11). Because Nathan had "missed it" once before, David could have become defensive and critical of Nathan's prophetic ministry, citing the earlier mistake as an excuse for disregarding Nathan's rebuke. Yet David quickly received Nathan's correction instead, indicating that his prophetic authority had not been diminished by his one recorded mistake. David recognized that Nathan was still being sent to him by God with divine authority and approval, and the prophet ministered correction to the king as the mouthpiece of God.

Disciples at Tyre Prophesy to Paul. When Paul was headed back to Jerusalem from Asia on his final missionary journey, he stopped in Tyre to visit the believers there. The Scripture tells us that these disciples "said to Paul through the Spirit that he should not go up to Jerusalem" (Acts 21:4).

The primary purpose of this trip was to take a large offering to the church at Jerusalem from the believers in other cities (Acts 24:17, Rom.15:27). Paul surely could have sent this money by another's hands, particularly after having been warned repeatedly of the dangers awaiting him in Jerusalem. But this was in Paul's eyes a special offering with a special destination, coming from the predominantly Gentile believers to whom Paul had ministered.

This particular offering showed the Jewish leaders in a tangible way the gratitude of the Gentile believers toward those among whom the gospel had originated. Paul was not only bringing financial assistance; he was declaring unity in the midst of a continuing mutual misunderstanding between Jewish and Gentile believers that plagued the early Church. So his willingness to take the offering personally was a self-sacrificial mark of true spiritual fatherhood in the Body of Christ.

With this godly goal in mind, we see that Paul was convinced his decision to go to Jerusalem was of the Holy Spirit. He had previously stated of this mission that he went "bound in the Spirit unto Jerusalem" (Acts 20:22). So why did the disciples at Tyre say "through the Spirit" that he should not go? (The ramifications of this particular prophetic dilemma are discussed in more detail under question #7).

Human Application Added to Divine Revelation. Personally, I believe that these Christians had truly received a revelation from God, through the Spirit, that Paul would suffer if he went to Jerusalem. That much was accurate. My personal experience and knowledge of how pure revelation is received and then expressed by imperfect human vessels lets me know that they could have given their own application and interpretation of what had been revealed to them. Instead of simply saying that danger awaited Paul in Jerusalem, they told him he should not go. Thus their own understandable desire to protect him resulted in a heart-generated, rather than Holy Spirit-generated, **application** of what the Holy Spirit was seeking to express through them.

The Bible records no condemnation of these Christians in Tyre for their seemingly inaccurate interpretation. Paul did not send out a letter to his fellow ministers warning them to beware of any prophecies coming from the disciples at Tyre. Neither did the church at Tyre send out a report on Paul saying that he was self-willed and in rebellion against the prophetically revealed will of God. The people who prophesied were not stoned to death or labeled false prophets. Yet based on Paul's evaluation of their word—as evidenced by his response to it— they had "missed it" in delivering a personal prophecy.

Agabus' Prophecy to Paul. Some days after Paul received the word in Tyre, he received another word on his way to Jerusalem from the prophet Agabus, whom he encountered at Caesarea. This New Testament prophet took Paul's belt, bound his own hands and feet with it, and said: "So shall the Jews in Jerusalem bind the man who owns this (belt), and shall deliver him into the hands of the Gentiles" (Acts 21:11).

Within this prophecy are two particular details that appear not to have been fulfilled literally according to the biblical narrative. The first involves the word "bind," which in the Greek here means to bind, tie or be in bonds. The second involves the Greek word translated "deliver," which means to surrender, yield up or transmit. Critical to the sense of this latter word is the idea of actively, consciously and willingly handing over someone or something to someone else; it is employed that way in all the other one hundred and nineteen instances of its use in the New Testament.

When we read later in Acts what happened to Paul at Jerusalem (vv. 17-40), we find that these two details are inaccurate. The Jews in fact did not bind Paul and turn him over to the Romans. Instead, the Romans took him from them and bound him themselves (v. 33), "rescuing" him from them against their will, as the Roman captain also reported afterward in a letter to the governor (Acts 23:27).

Was It Accurate? We should note that it was the habit of biblical writers to mention the specific fulfillment of a prophecy, as in fact Luke did when the same prophet Agabus, on another occasion, correctly predicted the coming of a famine (Acts 11:28). Yet Luke records the events of Paul's arrest in Jerusalem in Acts 22 without comment.

If the word was inaccurate, what about the ability and obligation of the elders at Caesarea to judge the prophecy? Among those present were the evangelist Philip, his four prophetically perceptive daughters, and a number of other elders who travelled with Paul (Acts 20:4). Shouldn't we expect that they would have responded if they discerned that a prophet was speaking a wrong word to their apostle?

The situation is further confused by the fact that Paul later reported to the Jewish leaders at Rome that he was "delivered (the same Greek word) as a prisoner from Jerusalem into the hands of the Romans" (Acts 28:17). If the prophecy's use of the word "deliver" was inaccurate, then why does Paul himself describe the event that way?

Perhaps the best lesson to be learned from this situation is that we should avoid dissecting every little "jot and tittle" of a prophetic word to determine its accuracy. Such details as the ones that were seemingly inaccurate in Agabus' prophecies may make little difference in the overall point God is trying to make. So we should not be quick to judge a prophecy as inaccurate simply on the basis of insignificant points.

Humility and Accountability. Since all prophetic ministers are fallible and liable to make mistakes, our best strategy is to cultivate a spirit of humility as we minister that invites investigation and correction. We should also maintain accountable relationships with a spiritual overseer and with other leaders in the Body of Christ.

All personal prophecies at CI-NPM conferences are recorded. That way the person prophesying can be held accountable for what was said, and the people who heard the prophecy can be held accountable for misinterpreting, misapplying or failing to remember correctly what they have heard.

In addition, whenever CI-NPM members minister outside their own church or organization, they are required to leave an evaluation form with the senior minister or host minister there. This confidential form is then mailed directly to the bishop of the network for review. We believe that these two safeguards contribute to an effective system of accountability for dealing with inaccurate words.

Following through on Seemingly Inaccurate Words. The proper follow-up to an inaccurate word depends to a great extent on the time, place and setting in which the word was given. If given in a local church, for example, proper follow-up should involve the local eldership, the prophetic minister and his or her spiritual oversight, and the person receiving the prophecy.

If the audience that heard the inaccurate word was local rather than national, there should be no reason for giving national attention to the incident when following up on it. But if the word was published nationally in print or on a broadcast, then there needs to be a public follow-up with the same audience.

What Is the Motive? The motive for such follow-up should be examined. Does the prophecy need follow-up to help the person who received it? If confusion and doubt resulted from the prophecy, counseling may well be called for. On the other hand, there may be other, less helpful, motives. For example, is someone simply trying to prove to the prophet that he or she was off target?

The Scripture says, "Receive not an accusation against an elder, except in the mouth of two or three" (1Tim.5:19). This is for the protection of leaders who could be slandered with false reports. We should be cautious about receiving too readily an accusation against someone's personal sexual morality or financial integrity; in the same way, we should avoid slandering someone's ministry by declaring he or she gave a false prophecy when the facts do not absolutely substantiate the accusation. And even when an inaccurate word has been substantiated, follow-up should always be handled by mature believers who understand that God's purpose for discipline is redemptive and conciliatory.

If an inaccurate prophecy is dealt with publicly in a local church, the congregation should be provided with a balanced perspective that sets the word in the context of the prophet's ministry as a whole. If the people are told about all the accurate prophecies and quality ministry which may have taken place in addition to the one inaccurate word, some may be prevented from developing an attitude of distrust toward a true prophet of God.

2. WHAT ABOUT PROPHECIES THAT SEEM TO CONTRADICT ONE ANOTHER?

When we look at the Messianic prophecies in the Old Testament, we can readily see why God's people may have been confused or doubtful about some of them. Some of the words prophesying Jesus' life and ministry seemed on the surface to be contradictory or even mutually exclusive.

For example, the prophet Micah said the Messiah would be born in Bethlehem (Micah 5:2), yet the prophet Isaiah said His light would shine out of Galilee of the Gentiles (Is.9:1,2). In addition, the prophet Hosea predicted that God's Son would come out of Egypt (Hos.11:1). The resulting confusion caused some people to doubt Jesus' messiahship (John 7:41-43). Which of these prophecies was true?

As it turned out, of course, all of them were genuine prophecies fulfilled by Jesus' life. But only after it all happened was it clear how these seeming contradictory words could all be true.

Sometimes surface facts seem to contradict the accuracy of a prophecy or the validity of its fulfillment. The Pharisees and theologians, for example, declared that Jesus could not be the fulfillment of the prophecies concerning the true Prophet-Messiah, for there were no prophecies about His being born and raised in Nazareth of Galilee. So the surface information they knew caused them to reject Jesus.

The hidden fact of the matter, however, was that He was actually born in Bethlehem of Judea, which was in accordance with the Messianic prophecies. So the presumption of the Pharisees and others led them to miss the fulfillment of prophecy when it took place.

We have seen that God judges prophets for giving presumptuous prophecies. What then will He do to those who presumptuously declare true prophecies to be false?

Suffering Servant or Conquering King? We can take a second example from the Messianic prophecies. The prophet Isaiah said that the Messiah would be a suffering Servant, wounded, beaten and killed on our behalf (Is.53:4-9). The prophet Daniel, however, foresaw that the Messiah, whom he called the Son of Man, would come in clouds of glory as a conqueror and liberator (Dan.7:13-14). The seeming gap between these two pictures of the Messiah caused even more people to stumble in their understanding of Jesus. If the Messiah was supposed to come in power, how could Jesus be the Messiah?

Again, as it turns out, both prophetic pictures are true. But to fulfill them, the Messiah must come twice: the first time as a suffering Servant, the second as a conquering King. The mindset people had in Jesus' day prevented many from accepting Him because the reality about the Messiah was more complicated than they had anticipated, even though prophecy had predicted both comings of the Lord.

It Takes Patience to Procure Progressive Personal Prophecies. I have witnessed those who became discouraged with their prophecies or even rejected them because of seeming confusion, contradiction, or only partial fulfillment. To avoid such discouragement, we must keep in mind an important principle of prophetic proclamations: Not all the statements made within a single prophetic flow of words will necessarily be fulfilled in the order spoken or within a single time frame.

Consider, for example, Isaiah's flow of prophetic words about the ministry of the Messiah, recorded in Isaiah 61:1-2:

The Spirit of the Lord God is upon me; because the Lord hath anointed me to preach good tidings unto the meek; he hath sent me to bind up the brokenhearted, to proclaim liberty to the captives, and the opening of the prison to them that are bound; To proclaim the acceptable year of the Lord, ...and the day of vengeance of our God....

Jesus read this prophecy aloud in the synagogue and declared that He was fulfilling it (see Luke 4:16-21).

Nevertheless, Jesus did not quote the whole flow of the prophecy. He actually stopped in the middle of a sentence, because the part of the prophecy He was fulfilling in His first coming stopped at the phrase "to proclaim the acceptable year of the Lord." A subsequent portion of that sentence—"and the day of vengeance of our God"—applies to Him as well, but it is not to be fulfilled until Christ's second coming as judge of the earth. Thus even within a single sentence of prophecy, two events thousands of years apart are predicted.

The Pharisees could have accused Jesus of not properly quoting and applying the Messianic prophecy according to their own rigid interpretation and application of it. They could easily have said, "But what about 'the day of vengeance of our God'? Why did you leave that out? We don't see you pronouncing divine judgment on the world, and if you're not fulfilling all the statements of this prophecy together, then it must not apply to you."

Today, knowing as we do that Jesus' second coming will bring "the day of vengeance of our God," we can see that such an accusation by the Pharisees would only have reflected their own limited understanding and experience of the prophetic process. They would have rejected the idea that Isaiah's prophecy accurately applied to Jesus because they didn't know that two thousand years lay between the two parts of that single prophetic sentence.

The same was true of the flow of prophetic statements that the angel Gabriel prophesied personally to Mary, the mother of Jesus:

> And, behold, thou shalt conceive in thy womb, and bring forth a son, and shalt call his name JESUS. He shall be great, and shall be called the Son of the Highest; and the Lord God shall give unto him the throne of his father David: And he shall reign over the house of Jacob for ever; and of his kingdom there shall be no end (Luke 1:31-33).

Several of these statements, though spoken all on the same occasion, apply to a different time and season of fulfillment. The prophetic word about Mary's conception was fulfilled immediately. The word about Jesus' birth took place later in the normal, natural season of nine months after conception. And the statements about Jesus' eternal kingdom are even now still to be completely fulfilled.

With these examples in mind, we should remember that just as we should not too quickly judge prophecies as inaccurate, neither should we rush to label them contradictory. We may simply not have sufficient information to make the judgment. Time and experience may well prove, as they did with the Messianic prophecies, that prophetic words only **appear** to be contradictory. Those that seem mutually exclusive today may well show themselves complementary as God works things out in His timing.

Life Has Different Seasons. Keep in mind as well that life has its seasons, each one unique. One prophecy may refer to one season in a person's life, and another prophecy to another season. So if one word, for example, talks about financial abundance, while another predicts lean times, they probably do not contradict, but rather describe different time periods in the future.

Also be careful of reading too much into words. Sometimes the contradictions are actually in our **assumptions** about what prophetic utterances say, not in what they truly say.

For example, one prophecy may say that a man is called to be a prophet, while another says he has a pastor's heart, and yet another predicts that he will do the work of an evangelist. Besides the obvious possibility that these three ministries might take place in different seasons of his life, we should note as well that having "a pastor's heart" is not the same as being called to the office of pastor, nor is "doing the work of an evangelist" the same as being called as an evangelist. If we assume that three different kinds of five-fold ministry callings have been prophesied over the same person, we may conclude that the prophecies contradict one another. But if we pay close attention to what was actually said, the seeming contradictions will disappear.

For example, if I had received a number of prophecies from different people when I was a teenager, and each prophecy had described a different aspect of the various ministries I was to have during the following forty years, I might have been confused or thought the prophets were contradicting one another. One could have prophesied that I would pastor; another, that I would teach; another, that I would be a prophet; and yet another, that I would do an apostolic work. I might have received words about traveling ministry and ministering in one place, about financial setbacks and financial prosperity, and on and on.

At that age and stage of my life, I might have cried out in despair: "What is my five-fold ministry calling? Will I have a local or worldwide ministry? Will I be popular or persecuted, limited in my resources or financially blessed?

Nevertheless, all those prophetic words would have been accurate in describing one season of my life or another. I was a pastor for six years and a teacher at a Bible college for five years. I've done the apostolic work of founding and building Christian International College and the Network of Prophetic Ministries. Meanwhile, throughout my whole ministerial life I have functioned as a prophet.

If you receive a number of prophecies which seem confusing and contradictory, don't despair or throw the prophecies away. Just allow time and life experience to prove their accuracy.

3. DOES PROPHECY NORMALLY COME TO PASS ACCORDING TO HUMAN EXPECTATIONS?

Christ was the fulfillment of hundreds of Old Testament prophecies. Yet men and women in their natural understanding of those prophecies found it difficult to receive Him as the Messiah (John 6:41, 10:24). For that reason, we must conclude that a natural mind-set alone is not sufficient to determine when a prophecy has been fulfilled. We must have a divinely-given spirit of revelation—just as we must have to discern rightly the meaning of the Scripture.

Take another biblical example. The New Testament writers declared by the spirit of revelation that certain Old Testament prophecies were fulfilled by events that at times totally contradicted merely natural thinking and circumstances.

The first Pentecost provides a helpful illustration. Peter spoke by revelation when he described that day as an event "spoken of by the prophet Joel" concerning the outpouring of the Holy Spirit (Acts 2:16). Meanwhile, those without the revelation saw the same event yet asked, "What meaneth this?" (vv. 12,13). This was a historical event without precedent, fulfilling prophecy—but many did not perceive its importance and so missed out on its benefits.

Isaiah the prophet predicted destruction for Israel, saying that through the Babylonian invasion God would speak in judgment to His people "with stammering lips and another tongue" (Is.28:11). This in fact had a literal fulfillment in history. Yet Paul took that prophecy and applied it to describe the gift of tongues given by the Holy Spirit to the Church (1Cor.14:21). Though the apostle's application may seem to the natural mind to be out of context and hermeneutically incorrect, yet we must accept his interpretation as valid and divinely revealed because it is part of the New Testament scriptures.

A Personal Example. On a much smaller scale, my own life provides several clear illustrations of how prophecies often come to pass in ways other than what we ourselves envision. Once, for example, I went to a minister for prophecy, extending my faith for an assurance from God that He would supply a desperate financial need. It was two days after a $40,000 payment was due. A statement in the prophecy I received said, "I will supply your need, for to deny you would be to deny Myself." So I went away confessing that my financial need was met. But as it turned out, that payment was never made.

What happened? I told the Lord that He had not fulfilled His prophetic promise to me.

God replied, "Yes, I did. I met the need I promised to meet prophetically through my servant. The problem is that **you** thought your greatest need was that payment. But **I** saw an even greater need than that money, and I have met that need faithfully." He then enlightened my mind so I could see how much greater was the need He **did** meet that night, and I had learned again an old lesson: Prophetic fulfillment does not always come according to our desires and expectations.

4. WHY DOES GOD ALLOW FALSE PROPHETS AND PROPHECY TO BE MANIFESTED?

We might answer that question with a series of other questions, whose answers are all the same: Why does God allow false teachers and teachings? Why are there heresies and cults? Why are there charlatans and frauds in the Church?

The biblical reply to those questions is that God allows false ministry for several reasons. First, He allows it to test the hearts of His people:

> If there arise among you a prophet, or a dreamer of dreams, and giveth thee a sign or a wonder, and the sign or wonder come to pass, whereof he spoke unto thee, saying, Let us go after other gods, which thou hast not known, and let us serve them, thou shalt not hearken unto the words of that prophet, or that dreamer of dreams; **for the Lord your God proveth you,** to know whether ye love the Lord your God with all your heart and with all your soul (Deut.13:1-3).

Such divine tests demonstrate whether God's people will follow Him or chase after some miracle worker who draws them away from His commandments and will.

Second, God allows the false to appear because the contrast between the true and the false provides an opportunity to discern the differences clearly, and to highlight what is true: "There must needs be heresies among you, that those which are approved might be made manifest" (1Cor.11:19).

Third, God allows the false to arise as a source of delusion and deception for those who are dishonest: "Furthermore, since they did not think it worthwhile to retain the knowledge of God, he gave them over to a depraved mind, to do what ought not to be done" (Rom.1:28).

Judgment and Separation. Fourth, God uses the false to bring judgment on the disobedient. Jeremiah tells us that in his day false prophets had multiplied among God's people, causing them to err and leading them into immorality. But they became a tool in God's hand for judging the wickedness of His people, because they falsely predicted peace when in fact God was planning to overthrow the nation (see Jer.23:9-40).

Finally, God allows the false to appear among His people so that He can separate those who are committed to His purposes from those who are merely curious about what is taking place. You can be sure that when the religious leaders of Jesus' day rose against Him, speaking falsely and causing controversy, many who had followed Him up to that point simply to see the miracles consequently fell away instead of pressing in to know for certain what was true. In a similar way, I believe that the controversy now swirling around prophetic ministry will sharply increase in the days to come, because God never makes it easy to come into present truth. As with Gideon's army, the group of 22,000 who are faint-hearted and easily discouraged over imbalance, extremes and error will have ample opportunity to "go home" and give up on the whole movement because of the problems of a few.

5. HOW CAN WE WEIGH AND PROVE A WORD TO BE TRUE YET HAVE FAITH IN THE WORD OF THE LORD AND BELIEVE HIS PROPHETS?

In trying to respond faithfully yet responsibly to personal prophecy, we sometimes encounter a dilemma. On the one hand, the scriptural attitude toward receiving prophecy is positive. We are told to "despise not prophesyings" (1Thess.5:20). We are encouraged to believe God's prophets in order to prosper (2Chr.20:20). And we learn that God's word will not profit us if it is not "mixed with faith" in our hearts as we receive it (Heb.4:2).

On the other hand, the Scriptures warn us that not all words claiming to be from God are truly Holy Spirit-inspired. In the verse immediately following Paul's exhortation not to despise prophetic utterances, he cautions, "Prove all things" (1Thess.5:21). When the apostle reminds the Corinthians that all may prophesy, he notes that their words should nevertheless be judged (1Cor.14:31,29). We cannot naively assume that every pronouncement claiming prophetic authority should be believed without question.

A Sharp Dilemma. The dilemma is sharpened when the word, if true, calls for action on the part of the hearer. For example, in the Old Testament, God once commanded a young prophet to go from Judah to Bethel and prophesy there against King Jeroboam's false altar dedicated to idols (see 1Kings 13:1-32). Then, the Lord said, he was to return home by a different route without stopping to eat or drink along the way.

Nevertheless, an old prophet from Bethel met him on the road and lied to him, saying that an angel had instructed him to tell the young prophet he was to come to the old man's house to dine. The young prophet believed the word was from God, did as the old man said—and died under the judgment of God for disobedience. His gullibility destroyed him.

A Prophesied Famine. An opposite example comes from the New Testament when the prophet Agabus prophesied at Antioch that the world would suffer a drought and famine. The disciples in the church there who heard that word had a choice: They could act on the word in faith and obedience by taking up a relief offering to send to the church in Judea. Or they could wait to see if the word truly came to pass—and if it did, they would have missed the opportunity to respond.

Apparently these early believers at Antioch were gifted with discernment and had a corporate witness both to Agabus and his prediction. They moved in faith according to the word he had spoken, and the prophecy did in fact come to pass (see Acts 11:27-30).

Tidal Wave in Florida? To take a more recent example, in the late 1970's a woman prophesied that the nation of Guatemala would suffer an earthquake. It came to pass just at the time she had predicted. So when a little while later she prophesied that the state of Florida would be inundated by a great tidal wave on a particular date, you can understand why some Christians in Florida were apprehensive as the day approached. Since the woman's previous word had been accurate, they asked, should they act on this latter word by getting out of Florida?

One particular church was trying to get the mind of the Lord on the matter, and they asked me to confirm or disconfirm the prophecy. I sought God for clarity on the matter, and heard Him say that there would be no tidal wave. I reported this to the church, and after the elders had taken counsel together, they decided to stay put. The tidal wave never came.

Two Precautions. What should we do in a similar situation? To avoid the deception of false prophecies, we can take two precautions. First, we can become educated and mature in the Scriptures and the Spirit to exercise discernment based on biblical truth and an inner witness. There is simply no substitute for spiritual maturity and biblical understanding.

When we have a close relationship with Jesus, then we will know the voice of the Shepherd. Even if our minds do not understand a prophetic word, our spirit will be able to accept or reject it. We can learn to trust our own spirit's inner witness, both to the prophecy itself and to the spirit of the one prophesying.

Jesus said that sheep know the voice of their own shepherd, and His sheep know His voice (see John 10:1-16). But sheep aren't born knowing the voice of their shepherd. They learn to recognize it through a continuing relationship of hearing and responding to him. The same is true of our relationship to our Shepherd.

Second, we must be under the covering authority of spiritual eldership that can speak into our lives with authority and offer wise counsel about the prophecies we receive. Our pastor and other leaders can help us determine whether a prophecy is scriptural, accurate and timely.

Christians should not be gullible or naive, believing every word that anyone speaks in the name of the Lord. False prophets will undoubtedly arise, telling some people to divorce their spouses, advising others to make disastrous or unethical business deals, encouraging still others to act in a variety of ungodly ways. If we "prove" prophetic words by submitting them to Scripture and spiritual overseers, God will not judge our response as a lack of faith; He will honor it as wise obedience to His directives in Scripture.

Knowing that false prophets will appear, Christians should nevertheless not allow themselves to be plagued by skepticism or cynicism so that they doubt even true words from the Lord. That attitude would only render them hesitant and indecisive, ultimately robbing them of God's promises (see Heb.3:18,19).

6. WILL THE PERSON RECEIVING A TRUE PROPHETIC WORD ALWAYS HAVE A WITNESS IN HIS OR HER SPIRIT THAT IT IS ACCURATE AND FROM GOD?

The inner witness of the Spirit with our spirit is one way of determining that a prophetic utterance is of the Lord: "The Spirit itself beareth witness with our spirit, that we are the children of God" (Rom.8:16). Nevertheless, it is probably the most subjective way to discern true prophecy, since our "witness" can be clouded by our previous prejudices or ways of thinking, incorrect knowledge, or failure to know what is in our own heart. Every person has blind spots.

The prophet Jeremiah said that the heart is deceitful above all things, so that we have difficulty in truly knowing it. For that reason, we should not discard a word as inaccurate or incorrect simply because we do not "witness" to it. (How to determine a true witness in our spirit is covered in more detail in the first two volumes of this series.)

Elisha and Hazael. The prophet Elisha once prophesied to Hazael, a military commander under king Ben-Hadad of Aram, that the soldier would one day torch the cities of Israel and commit horrible atrocities against its people, such as murdering the babies and ripping open the pregnant women. Hazael responded with surprise, saying that he could never do that sort of thing. He did not feel that he was capable of such degradation; he did not think such a thing could be in his heart (see 2Kings 8:7-15). Peter gave a similar reaction when Jesus spoke a personal prophecy that he would deny Him.

Nevertheless, when Elisha also prophesied that Hazael would be the next king of Aram, Hazael went to King Ben-Hadad, who was seriously ill, and suffocated him. After that cruel assassination, he did in fact become king and went on to oppress the people of Israel throughout his reign, just as the prophet had spoken (2Kings 13:22). Apparently, murder was in Hazael's heart when Elisha prophesied to him, but he himself did not recognize that reality and thought the prophet had spoken wrongly. He was deceived by his own heart and thus was unable to witness to a true prophetic word.

We Do Not Know Our Own Hearts. One of our CI-NPM members recalls giving a word to a man about his need to get rid of a root of bitterness in his heart by forgiving someone. The man reacted sharply, insisting that he loved everyone and held nothing against anyone. Nevertheless, when he counseled later with the prophetic minister, it came out that he had indeed made severe judgments against several people and had failed to forgive them. Though he had thought he knew his own heart, he had not immediately recognized the problem, even when he was directly confronted with it.

I will never forget one time when I was prophesying in a local church to a man whose pastor was standing directly behind him as I ministered. As the word of the Lord began to deal with certain problems in his character and temperament, the man began to frown and shake his head, as if to say, "No, no, no!" But at the same time, his pastor was standing behind him smiling and vigorously nodding his head, as if to say, "Yes, yes, yes!" The pastor knew the man's heart better than the man himself.

7. IS PROPHETIC MINISTRY ALWAYS THE PURE WORD OF THE LORD, OR DOES IT SOMETIMES CONTAIN A MIXTURE OF HUMAN OPINIONS, APPLICATIONS OR INTERPRETATIONS?

Both the biblical record and my experience with numerous prophetic ministers indicate that those who prophesy may sometimes mix the pure word of the Lord with their own ideas. Only God is infallible! One possible scriptural example is a situation we discussed earlier—Paul's last journey to Jerusalem and the prophetic warnings he received on the way.

On that journey, Paul told the Ephesian elders, "And now, compelled by the Spirit, I am going to Jerusalem, not knowing what will happen to me there. I only know that in every city the Holy Spirit warns me that prisons and hardships are facing me" (Acts 20:22,23 NIV). In this and other passages (Rom.15:25-31; Acts 19:21), Paul indicated that he firmly believed this journey and its consequences in Jerusalem were the will of God for him, despite the adversities that would be involved. Nevertheless, the disciples at Tyre told Paul "through the Spirit" that he should not make the trip (Acts 21:4).

What happened? Is the same Holy Spirit expressing a set of opposite prophetic directives for the same person and situation? How do we reconcile Paul's statement that he was **"compelled by the Spirit"** to go to Jerusalem with the statement that the disciples at Tyre had warned him **"through the Spirit"** that he should not go?

God's Testing. We can suggest a couple of possible solutions to the puzzle. One might be that the Holy Spirit inspired the disciples at Tyre to tell Paul not to go to Jerusalem as a way of testing his commitment to fulfill God's purposes for him despite the threat of suffering, persecution, prison and death. There are in fact biblical precedents that reveal the possibility of God's giving us the option to do less than His highest purpose for our lives.

For example, God and Elijah wanted Elisha to receive and carry on Elijah's prophetic ministry. But Elijah gave Elisha three options and opportunities to stop short of receiving that prophetic mantle. Jesus gave the same choice to the Twelve when other disciples began leaving Him; He asked them, "Will ye also go away?" (John 6:67). And Gideon, through God's directive, gave his 32,000 soldiers the chance to go home instead of doing battle. Some 22,000 chose not to go all the way with Gideon and with God.

Numerous scriptural texts tell us that God tests, tries, checks out and proves the righteous. The first personal prophecy Paul received after his conversion declared that he would suffer great things for the cause of Christ and His Church. So the disciples at Tyre may well have been instruments of God for testing Paul's dedication to fulfill his original prophecy.

A Mix of God-Inspired and Merely Human Words. Another explanation of the seeming contradiction between what Paul heard from God and what the disciples at Tyre heard from God would reckon it to be an example of how Spirit-inspired and human-inspired words can be intermingled in one prophetic expression. Perhaps what the disciples actually received through the Spirit was the same word Paul and others had received about the impending danger for Paul in Jerusalem. Yet because of their love for Paul, the disciples may have gone on to add to that pure word their own interpretation and application, telling him not to go (his travelling companions had already urged him in a similar way, Acts 21:11).

Emotional involvement and personal desire are two circumstances that frequently hinder the pure expression of prophecy. So it's reasonable to guess that the Christians at Tyre may have allowed their own natural emotions and their assumptions about God's will for their friend to create an impure flow of the prophetic word.

Over many years of giving countless personal prophecies and working with numerous other prophets, I have discovered that it's certainly possible for such a mix of human thoughts and divine thoughts to take place. At times Christians can accurately sense something in their spirits while at the same time failing to receive a divine word of wisdom for properly applying and interpreting what they are sensing. It requires years of prophetic experience to gain the maturity and spiritual wisdom to rightly describe and properly apply our prophetic perceptions.

Contemporary Illustrations. To take a more recent example, I remember a situation in which one of our CI-NPM ministers prophesied to a man about the reconciliation of someone close to him. The one who was prophesying assumed that it meant a reconciliation in the man's marriage. He discovered later, however, that the word turned out to be speaking about a relationship with the man's brother, who was at odds with him in a "Jacob and Esau" situation.

The word was right, but the prophet's assumption about its application was wrong. If the prophet had given an interpretation and application based on his own thoughts, he would have mixed human interpretation with divine revelation—thereby diluting the purity and accuracy of the prophetic word. This is one cause of what I would call "presumptuous prophecy."

On another occasion, a "prophet in training" was praying for a woman who had just lost a child in an accident and was grieving and feeling guilty over it. The man prophesying did not know about the tragedy, but he saw in the Spirit a picture of an empty swing set and the mother looking on with a sense of loss and pain. He then went on to interpret the picture on his own. He said he believed the picture meant that the woman had lost her first love for Jesus and that God wanted her to return to it.

This man gave the right revelation but the wrong interpretation, and consequently his words failed to minister life to the woman. If we would avoid such situations ourselves, we must always remember when we prophesy to share exactly what we see or sense in the Spirit without adding an interpretation or application out of our own thinking.

8. ARE PROPHETS DIVINELY GIFTED BY GOD TO MINISTER PROPHETICALLY TO ANYONE WHO COMES BEFORE THEM FOR SUCH MINISTRY?

The prophet is one of the five-fold ministries in which Christ has invested a particular anointing that abides with the person (Eph.4:11). The giftings of God are **given**, not lent for special occasions. Christ's gifts simply enable the human spirit to operate within the ability of Christ.

Pastors, for example, do not need a special unction to preach every Sunday; rather, they simply plan to preach and share the truth God places on their heart. They are shepherds to their sheep twenty-four hours a day, regardless of when the phone rings or what the need is. As pastors they must be ready to minister "in season and out of season" (2Tim.4:2).

Ministering by Faith. In the same way, the prophet's anointing abides and can be drawn from by faith in Christ to give a word to individuals in need—whenever and wherever they are. Like all ministers, the prophet must "use whatever gift he has received to serve others, faithfully administering God's grace in its various forms," including "speaking the very words of God" (1Pet. 4:10,11 NIV).

Paul tells us that "if a man's gift is prophesying, let him use it in proportion to his faith" (Rom. 12:6 NIV). Every divine attribute and ability—prophecy included—is received, activated and ministered by faith. So when someone comes before a prophet needing ministry, the prophet can simply prophesy by faith, trusting that Christ's abiding gift is available. Nevertheless, if a novice in the prophetic ministry envisions him or herself as having more faith and prophetic ability than is actually the case, that person is likely to give many presumptuous prophecies while trying to prophesy "by faith" in their own gifting.

Spirits of the Prophets Are Subject. At the same time, Paul tells us that "the spirits of prophets are subject to the control of prophets" (1Cor.14:32 NIV). The situation that occasioned this remark was the need for prophets at Corinth to take turns in speaking, but I believe it reveals the general reality that the prophets' spirits can be subjected to their wills, both for restraint as well as for activation.

If this is the case, then we need to avoid religious regulations on the prophetic word that attempt to limit God. Some folks, for example, claim we can only prophesy if we first have some particular feeling or physical sensation. Others insist that only five to ten people maximum can receive prophetic ministry in any given service.

In fact, when I was ministered to by a prophetic presbytery in Bible college back in 1953, over eighty students had fasted for three days in preparation to receive a prophetic word. They and a number of other Christians hungry to hear God's word were present at the meeting. Yet the prophetic presbytery only called out two people, ministered to them, and then closed the service, feeling that the Holy Spirit was finished despite the many who did not receive ministry.

On the other hand, my experience and the experience of the prophetic ministers I have trained, teaches us that we can draw on Christ's abiding gift by faith whenever we need it.

I am able to prophesy over anyone I lay hands on because of the divine gifting to a prophet—God's grace and faith to flow prophetically in this manner. Paul said that we are to prophesy according to the **proportion** of our faith (Rom.12:6). All prophets and prophetic people are not gifted the same way, nor do they have the same amount of faith for ministering spiritual things.

When I was first activated and released in prophetic ministry at the age of 17, I only had faith to prophesy congregational prophecies. After a particular prophetic message was spoken over me the next year, a greater anointing was activated in me. My exposure to personal prophecy increased my faith to prophesy to individuals now and then. But my faith and experience in prophetic ministry was limited to ministering with other prophetic ministers in prophetic presbyteries and occasionally giving personal prophecies to individuals.

Nearly a decade later, however, God sovereignly moved upon me in a meeting one night and enabled me to prophesy personally to all eighty-five people present. At the time I thought that was a once-in-a-lifetime experience, but two weeks later in another meeting I prophesied to one hundred and fifty people. For the next ten years that new understanding of prophetic ministry allowed me the faith and ability to practice it, and in 1979 I began training others to do the same.

To try to explain in detail how we are able to prophesy by faith at any given time is as difficult for me to try to explain the technicalities of how I am able to speak in my spirit prayer language anywhere and anytime I will to do so (1Cor.14:14). No doubt all prophets have not had the same experience, nor have they been activated into this type of prophetic flow. But the differences in prophetic ministry don't make any of us greater or lesser prophets or prophetic people. We just are what we are and do what we do by the grace of God.

(For a further discussion of this topic, see pp. 66-76 of volume 2 in this series, *Prophets and the Prophetic Movement*.)

9. IS IT POSSIBLE TO PROPHESY A PERSON'S DESIRE IF THE DESIRE IS IN CONFLICT WITH GOD'S WILL FOR THAT PERSON'S LIFE?

This question raises some difficult issues, yet it must be addressed. We may be disturbed at the prospect of God sometimes having (or at least allowing) a prophet to speak the fulfillment of someone's desire even when the fulfillment is not His best for that person. Yet the Scriptures indicate that at times He does precisely that.

We should note first a more general principle in the Bible that is clear whether or not prophetic ministry is involved: God sometimes gives us what we want, even when it is not best for us. This reality is evident in the parable of the prodigal son, where the father—who represents God the Father—gives his son his heritage prematurely, even though the father knew it would cause the son's downfall (Luke 15:11-31). In the same way, today we can insist on our spiritual heritage from God the Father before we are mature enough to handle it properly.

We can also find examples of this truth in the history of Israel. When the Israelites cried out for a king, God instructed Samuel to anoint one for them, even though it was clearly not His will (1Sam.8). The Lord wanted to feed His people only manna in the wilderness, yet they continually complained and lusted for meat. So He gave them meat until it "came out of their nostrils" and they loathed it (Num.11:4-34). And we have already discussed the example of Hezekiah, who begged for and received an extension of his life—to the sorrow of all Israel (2Kings 21:1-17).

Can a prophet actually prophesy the fulfillment of a human desire not in accordance with God's best? Isaiah apparently did just that to Hezekiah, as did Moses with the meat for the Israelites. And Samuel's anointing of Saul was done at God's bidding in the authority of the prophetic office. God had Moses prophesy the quail in abundance, and he had Samuel prophesy Saul's kingship; yet afterward, as these prophecies were being fulfilled, He sent judgment upon those who received and acted on the prophecies.

God Can Send a Delusion. Two scriptural texts in this regard are especially disturbing, one from the Old Testament and one from the New. God told Ezekiel to tell the elders of Israel:

> When any Israelite sets up idols in his heart and puts a wicked stumbling block before his face and then goes to a prophet, I the Lord will answer him myself in keeping with his great idolatry...And if the prophet is enticed to utter a prophecy, **I the Lord have enticed that prophet** (Eze.14:4-9 NIV).

The idols in the heart represent the willful, selfish desires that people persist in pursuing. This scriptural text seems to indicate that those who willfully disobey God yet seek prophetic ministry may well get a word "in keeping with" their idolatrous and selfish desires rather than in keeping with God's will.

In the New Testament, Paul says of those who "refused to love the truth": "For this reason **God sends them a powerful delusion** so that they will believe the lie" (2Thess.2:10,11 NIV). Though Satan is the father of lies, we find in this text an indication that God may at times arrange for rebellious people to hear a word that encourages them to believe the lie they already cherish.

This also seems to be the implication of the prophetic picture the prophet Micaiah described to the wicked King Ahab. On that occasion, the king had decided he wanted to attack Ramoth Gilead and was looking for prophets to give some kind of divine sanction to what he had already purposed in his heart to do. Micaiah saw in a heavenly vision God command a lying spirit to enter the false prophets and entice Ahab to his death by prophesying that he should go ahead and make the military move he desired (1Kings 22:19-23).

Prophetic Testing. Sometimes a prophecy will test our heart to see if we will twist it to fit our own selfish desires. The word itself may be true, but if our heart is wrong, we may take the word and abuse it for our own purposes. We subconsciously conclude, "This is what I want the prophecy to mean, so this is how I will interpret it."

For example, I once knew of a pastor who received a prophetic word that included a statement about having a "new ministry and a new family." The person prophesying assumed that the word meant the pastor's ministry and family would experience a season of spiritual and relational renewal. But the pastor himself, who was having an affair with his female worship leader, went home, divorced his wife, and married the other woman—claiming that God had confirmed what was already in his heart.

Perhaps the important thing for prophetic ministers to remember in light of this reality is that we must be careful not to speak beyond what we sense in the Spirit. Just because we get a word of knowledge, for example, about a couple's desire to get married or a pastor's hope for a new ministry is no reason to conclude that their desire is also God's desire. We should only confirm the desires of a person's heart when we hear clearly from God that He has put those desires in the person's heart.

10. WHAT WRONG MOTIVES MUST PROPHETS BE MOST CAREFUL TO AVOID IN MINISTRY?

I think Satan most often tempts prophetic ministers to be motivated by a desire either **for control** or for **personal gain**.

Human beings are free moral agents, and while God does give divine direction and confirmation through prophetic ministry, individuals are still responsible for making their own decisions without a spirit of control or manipulation influencing them. Christians should not look to prophetic ministers to tell them every detail of their life and ministry. Otherwise they will become dependent on other human beings and prophecies rather than dependent on God.

Witchcraft and Manipulation. The spirit of domination or control will sometimes be manifested by people who feel they have the right and responsibility to prophesy intricate details to others about whom to marry, how to spend or invest money, where to move, and other decisions. This normally occurs when one person presents him or herself as spiritually superior to others, convincing the "subordinates" that they need the "superior's" continual advice, counsel and prophetic perceptions to be in God's will.

Such domination may involve a prophetic minister dictating "orders" from God via prophecy, but it may also take other forms that do not involve prophetic ministry. For example, a pastor may lord it over the flock, attempting to make all their minor decisions. Even between Christian friends an extreme mentoring relationship may develop in which one person will do nothing without checking with the other.

Christians are vulnerable in this regard because the human race is divided into leaders and followers. Those who have the leader's personality profile are tempted to lead and control others by whatever means they have. Meanwhile, the followers are tempted to have the leaders take away from them the responsibility for making decisions.

Of course, this kind of unhealthy control is not true prophesying, pastoring or mentoring. It is rather witchcraft and manipulation under the guise of spiritual authority and ministry.

To avoid being controlled by unscrupulous Christians who use prophecy as a manipulative tool, believers need to remember that prophecy is only one way of determining the will of God for their lives. God will also confirm His direction by the

Scriptures, the peace of the Spirit, pastoral counsel, and providential circumstances. (See chapter 9 of *Prophets and Personal Prophecy* to discover the many biblical ways we can personally know God's Word, Will, and Way for our lives.)

From the perspective of the prophetic minister, it is good to remember that all prophetic words should be given in a spirit of humility and freedom. Even when we must administer correction, we should be low-key and approachable, offering wise adjustments and suggestions rather than thundering condemnations that may be intimidating rather than redemptive.

Ministering in a Local Church. When traveling prophets come to minister in a local church, what authority and scope of ministry do they have in that setting? Some people today are wrongly teaching that prophets and apostles have an authority that is superior to the other five-fold ministries, thus concluding that when a prophet goes into the local church he or she should in some sense be allowed to take charge of the church. I heard of at least one local church where a man came in, claimed to be God's prophet for the church, and proceeded to control the life of the congregation, dictating the church's governmental structure, who would be fired and hired, and changing its worship team. In effect, he replaced the senior pastor, who knew so little about the proper role of a prophet that he agreed to the arrangement because the prophet had "validated" his own authority by ministering some accurate words accompanied by healings.

This is a false view of the prophet's (or apostle's) authority that allows some people to dominate, dictate and control entire congregations. No doubt prophetic and apostolic ministries are foundational ministries (Eph.2:20), and God has thus anointed them to help in the foundational structuring or restructuring of churches when **invited** to do so. But keep in mind that the apostle Paul, even when writing to the church at Corinth that he had fathered, prefaced his apostolic correction with these words: "Not that we lord it over your faith, but we work with you for your joy" (2Cor.1:24 NIV).

Prophets and apostles invited in to minister to a local congregation must remember that they have not been called to "lord it over" the church, changing or rearranging whatever they like. They are there to help and serve, not to dominate or control.

I teach all our prophets and prophetic ministers that they are responsible to give the word of the Lord to the pastor and his congregation. But all words must be given under the covering and approval of the local pastor. If the prophetic words they feel led to give are radically corrective or directive, the words should be submitted to the pastor before speaking them publicly to the congregation.

This doesn't compromise the prophets' responsibility to speak for God, nor does it make them mere people-pleasers. God is the author of structure and delegated authority. He is never displeased by a prophet's ministering with and under established authority.

To use divine authority and ministry in a way that usurps divinely-established authority is unethical. A minister's "M's" of message and ministry may be in line, but if he or she undermines the church's appointed authority, the minister's "M's" of methods, manners, and maturity are out of order. There is a divine protocol in ministering the Word of the Lord to senior leadership in the local church or a national ministry.

A "Measure of Government." We should also keep in mind Paul's further remarks to the church at Corinth: "But we will not boast of things without our measure, but according to the measure of the rule which God hath distributed to us, a measure to reach even unto you" (2Cor.10:13). In other words, Paul was saying he had a measure of government, of rule, in his apostolic ministry, that included this particular church. In this church he had the God-given authority to exercise his gifting to set things in order. On the other hand, there were other churches in which he did not have that authority.

The same is true of our prophetic ministry. We will go into some churches and find an open door of authority to minister. The church leadership will welcome our prophetic insights into the needs and problems of the church because they recognize our gifting in that area.

In other churches, however, we are invited only to introduce the people to prophetic ministry. They do not want our insights about the church, or they may not even know we **have** insights about the church. In such a situation, it would be improper and unwise for us to tell the pastor all the things about the church that we sense could be changed and helped. Even though it would be a benefit to them, they would probably not be able to receive it because they would not have asked us in for that purpose. We would come across as dictatorial and dominating.

Personal Gain. True prophetic ministry will always glorify God in the life of the person receiving it. The spirit of prophecy is the testimony of Jesus (Rev.19:11), and the Holy Spirit was sent to glorify Jesus (John 16:14).

One way to check prophets' fruit is to notice whether their prophecies tend to promote themselves or their own ministries. Some have used the prophetic anointing to manipulate others into sending money to them. This is not only self-promotion; it borders on witchcraft and charlatanism. God's judgment on such blatant misrepresentation of His Spirit will be severe. Prophets must be trained by the Lord through life's circumstances to speak His word without the thought of either fear or favor of others—yet nevertheless with divine grace and maturity.

Avoid the Appearance of Self-Serving Words. Developing prophetic ministries would do well to shy away from giving words that could seem self-serving. This especially applies to the area of money and donations. I was ministering with a prophet one time to a woman who was rather wealthy. I did not know her, but the other prophet knew her quite well.

I perceived that God wanted this woman to sell a parcel of land, and that the Lord would reveal to her what to do with any profit from the sale. She responded by saying that God had been dealing with her about some land she had received as an inheritance, and that the word was a confirmation to her. Sadly enough, when the other prophet laid his hands on her and began to prophesy, he implied in what he said that God would direct her to give a large portion of money to a certain ministry with which she was already acquainted—that is, his own!

Another problem area in which ministers can manipulate for personal gain is decisions about church membership. Though it may be the will of God for a person to leave the church he or she currently attends and begin attending elsewhere, prophesying this will be seen by others as manipulation—especially if the church the person is being directed to join is the church of the prophetic minister. This is particularly the case because the reason God has most people change churches is to realize their untapped potential as a leader or as a major financial supporter.

The prophetic principle for prophesying direction or correction, and financial giving or receiving, is to refrain from prophesying in these areas to anyone about whom you have natural knowledge. Definitely do not prophesy any word that would bring self-promotion or self-confirmation, or that would advance any of your own self-interests. I don't know of any prophet or apostle on earth who could move long in this type of prophesying without falling into self-deception and wrongly motivated prophecies.

11. WHAT ARE PROPER GUIDELINES FOR MINISTERING PROPHETIC WORDS THAT DEAL WITH ROMANCE AND MARRIAGE?

We must remember that the marriage covenant is a life-long commitment between two people that needs to be entered with mutual desire and dedication—not under the stress or pressure of another person's prophetic perceptions. In addition, we should note that it is all too easy for those who are close to the person involved to be moved by natural desires and feelings, which may influence any word given. For these reasons, it is wise simply to avoid prophesying a particular marriage partner to others.

Many Christians believe that God has shown them who their mate will be. This may be true, but if so, the Holy Spirit will have to reveal it to the other person as well before there can be the unity and agreement necessary for a solid marriage foundation. Telling the other party "God told me you're to be my spouse" only leads to pressure and confusion, especially if the person who hears that claim is new in the Lord.

If the match is truly God's will, it will come to pass without manipulation or human schemes. The prophetic principle is that God always works on both parties separately, and generally in the same time frame, when He is the One who is truly directing the desires and spiritual impressions of those involved.

"Wishions." A man on our staff has counseled two single women who both say God told them they would marry the same well-known (and single) minister. One woman insisted that the fund-raising letters she received from his ministry office were written personally to her. She also claimed that in a meeting one time with thousands present, that particular minister looked at her from the platform with a "special look" that confirmed her conclusion.

The other woman firmly believed that the minister communicated with her by giving her messages in secret code and implied speech via other television evangelists whom she regularly watched. (Of course our staff member told her that idea was absurd, but she refused to believe him.) Yet she had never even so much as met the minister, shaken his hand, or talked with him.

Obviously, these women were so caught up in their desire to marry that they had deceived themselves into believing God had told them these things. I like to call these notions "wishions"—that is, wishful thinking manufactured into a "vision."

Occasionally there may be what can only be called a "prophetic marriage," in which God supernaturally speaks to both a man and woman about marrying each other. But these cases are extremely rare, and even then God clearly speaks to both parties involved.

Every Pentecostal or charismatic pastor I know who's single has had several young women in his church who are convinced God has told them they will marry him. I began pastoring when I was nineteen and single. Even though the congregation numbered only about sixty members, no less than six young ladies in that group became convinced through their "wishions" that I was destined to be their husband. Yet the young lady in the congregation whom I ended up marrying never once tried to initiate our romance and marriage through "wishions" or other spiritual directives.

A member of our board of governors has functioned for years as a single pastor over a congregation of thousands. He could talk to you for hours about the scores of women who have come up with weird ideas and strange behavior all in the name of "prophetic revelation" or "God told me/showed me…"

On the other hand, two members of our board of governors really did have a sovereignly, supernaturally, divinely and prophetically directed marriage. I know these couples well, and I can affirm that they entered into their marriages simply because God spoke to each of them about it independently and without the outside influence of others' prophesying. Nevertheless, they did follow through with the proper procedures of confirmations from parents, pastoral counsel, and confirmation from other credible sources.

You could say that truly prophetic marriages are planned in heaven and worked out on earth. But I've discovered that even marriages made in heaven can go through hell on earth for awhile until God brings romantic love, unity and maturity to the marriage. I wouldn't encourage anyone to seek a prophetic marriage. But if God sovereignly directs and confirms that way, then don't fear to enter into such a union. (See also chapter 8 in volume 1 of this series.)

12. WHAT ARE PROPER GUIDELINES FOR MINISTERING PROPHECIES TO THE SICK OR DYING CONCERNING THEIR HEALING?

It is the will of God for all to be saved and none to perish (1Tim.2:4). Nevertheless, in fact many perish every day without a saving knowledge of Christ. We cannot force people to be saved, nor pronounce that they are saved simply because of our strong conviction that God wants them saved.

In a similar way, healing for every sickness and disease was purchased by the thirty-nine stripes Jesus received, and it is the will of God to heal all who are sick (Is.53:5; Matt.8:16,17). Yet we cannot assume that any particular person will be healed, nor prophesy someone's healing simply because of our strong conviction that God wants them healed. Only when we receive a specific prophetic word of healing for a particular person should we prophesy healing for that person. Healing may be a true Logos word, but it may not be a rhema word that can be prophesied to that particular person at that particular time.

In addition, the prophetic minister should have not only a revelation of the sickness, but also the power to minister healing. One without the other is limited and ineffective. (For further discussion of this subject, see chapter 4 of the first volume in this series, *Prophets and Personal Prophecy*.)

13. IS THERE A NORMAL COURSE OF TIME FOR PROPHECY TO BE FULFILLED?

The word of the Lord to individuals—taken together as a whole as it is progressively manifested over time through multiple personal prophecies—normally requires for its complete fulfillment the context of the person's entire lifetime and even his or her heritage (descendants). It is rare for a prophecy about a person's ultimate call and ministry to be fulfilled in weeks, months, or even years.

Examples from David, Joseph, Abraham, and Saul. Biblical illustrations of this reality are numerous. For example, David was prophetically identified and anointed as Israel's next king while he was still a youth tending the sheep (1Sam.16:1-13). Yet he did not ascend the throne until the age of thirty, and the ultimate purposes of his kingly ministry were not fulfilled until many generations later, when his descendant Jesus was born to take his throne forever (Luke 1:30-33).

Joseph received prophetic dreams of his ministry and position when he was seventeen years old (Gen.37:1-9). But they did not come to pass until after he was thirty (Gen.41:46).

Abraham's prophecy of numerous descendants came when he was seventy-five years old (Gen.12:1-4), yet Isaac was born twenty-five years later (Gen.21:5), and the multitudes of descendants long after that. God's promise to give Abraham the land of Canaan were fulfilled centuries later through his heritage, the people of Israel, under Joshua.

Saul, who became the apostle Paul, received at the time of his conversion personal prophecy about his ministry from Ananias (Acts13:1,2). But he was not launched forth into his apostolic ministry until more than a decade later (Gal.1:15-18; Acts13:1-3).

These examples show clearly that God may take a lifetime and beyond to accomplish His purposes in and through us. So we should not be surprised if much of what has been prophesied over a person is still unfulfilled. I have only known one person who told me that all the personal prophecies she had ever received had come to pass—and she died three weeks after she made that statement. Only by the end of her life had all God's promises to her been fulfilled.

14. WILL PERSONAL PROPHECY REVEAL ALL OF GOD'S WILL FOR A PERSON'S ENTIRE LIFE?

Any given personal prophecy shows only one piece of the puzzle of God's will for a person's life. Paul told the Corinthians that "we prophesy in part" (1Cor.13:8). So a personal prophecy should not be accepted as the "last word" of God's plans nor as an all-inclusive view of the individual's life and ministry.

Abraham, for example, received eleven personal prophecies from God over the course of his lifetime of 175 years. Taken together, they progressively revealed God's ever-expanding purposes for him and provided increasing clarity to his call and purpose. (For a further discussion of this subject, see pp. 145-149 of the first volume in this series, *Prophets and Personal Prophecy*.)

This also means that if on a given occasion the prophetic words we receive do not address a particular matter, we cannot conclude that the matter is of no importance to God. If, for example, we are hoping for a word about financial provision, and instead we get a word about having another child, it may simply be the case that God's priority on that occasion was to prepare us for the child rather than comfort us about the provision He has planned. And if God does not reveal some hidden sin in our lives when we receive personal prophecy, we must conclude only that His mercy has spared us a little longer—not that He has decided to overlook or excuse our behavior (see Ex.4:24).

15. WHAT SHOULD BE THE RESULTS OF PROPHETIC MINISTRY?

Prophetic ministry can have a number of beneficial results for Christians. Overall, prophecy builds up the church by providing strength, encouragement and comfort to the saints (1Cor.14:3,12,26).

Prophets are foundation stones for building the local church, and their ministry can aid in the governmental structuring and restructuring of a congregation (Eph.2:20). They can also present to the local church divine revelation that will help it fulfill its mandate before God. Along with the other five-fold ministries, prophets have been given to the Church to equip believers for their own ministries and works of service (Eph.4:11,12). In particular, prophets can accomplish this equipping function by releasing and activating individuals into their ministries.

Avoid Harshness and Condemnation. In light of the redemptive, edifying function God has intended for prophetic ministry, we must avoid harsh, judgmental, critical words that will only condemn those who receive them. For example, I remember one occasion when a prophet declared publicly to a young man that he had a "dirty mind" and that he was "full of perversity." When the man began to cry—probably from humiliation—the prophet told him to be quiet and sit down.

Because the prophet's attitude was domineering and judgmental, the young man's situation was worsened rather than redeemed. The young man was so hurt, embarrassed and offended that he stopped going to church. So remember: It is God's **kindness** that leads people to repentance (Rom.2:4 NIV).

16. HOW ARE PROPHETS AND PROPHETIC MINISTRY TO RELATE TO THE REST OF THE BODY OF CHRIST?

According to the apostle Paul's instructions to the Corinthians, God has set prophets in the Church to function with and among other ministry gifts (1Cor.12:28). Prophets are not to be loners or to consider themselves too holy to associate with "normal" people. They are first of all disciples of Jesus Christ, profitable members of the Body of Christ, and then gifted ministries set in the Church.

When we look at the New Testament church in Antioch, we find that the prophets and teachers were first in relationship together within the congregation. Then they were sent out on missionary journeys from the local church according to God's direction (Acts 13:1). After each journey, they returned to the local church to report what had happened and to remain accountable.

Even the apostle Paul—who had been commissioned by the Lord Himself and had evidenced the signs of apostleship through signs, wonders, and new churches established—had a direct revelation from God that he was to be accountable in doctrinal matters to the elders at Jerusalem. He knew that even a mighty man or woman of God can run in vain if he or she ministers without relatedness, accountability and the witness of other leaders within the Church (see Gal.2:1,2,9).

Dangerous Traps. Exclusiveness and isolationism are tempting yet dangerous traps that prophets must avoid. Church history is full of sad examples of rebellious "Lone Ranger" prophets without a church covering who opened themselves to discouragement and deception. For that reason, true biblical accountability is a necessity for prophetic ministries.

In addition, prophetic words themselves must be recorded and given under proper authority so that those prophesying may be kept accountable. What I call "parking lot prophecies"— words given outside of the structures and settings that allow for accountability— should not be accepted as valid unless the person delivering them is willing to record them and have them judged by seasoned prophetic ministers.

17. WHAT IS A PROPER PROTOCOL FOR MINISTERING PERSONAL PROPHECY IN A PUBLIC SETTING?

We must be careful when ministering publicly to take care and exercise wisdom when revealing the details of a person's life. It can be difficult to minister in such a setting when the prophecy is addressing private matters that may embarrass the person receiving the word or expose someone's sin.

Usually, we can choose terms that allow the person to understand clearly what God is talking about without revealing specifics to those around or sounding critical and condemning. God will normally entrust such corrective words to mature prophetic ministers who can deliver His message in the spirit of healing and restoration God desires. Prophets who itch to prophesy judgment and to "straighten out" others are not candidates for this kind of ministry.

No Spiritual Gossip. Once I went to minister in a local church and I prophesied over one particular man. In the middle of the prophecy, I realized God was revealing that the man had a homosexual spirit and lifestyle, though not even the pastor was aware of it. I did not, however, come out and speak that specific revelation. Instead, I rebuked a spirit of uncleanness, and the man fell over physically and was delivered. Then I continued prophesying as before.

We must not assume that we are to share with everyone everything God says to us. That is only spiritual gossip. Sometimes the Lord tells us the secrets of other people's hearts so that we can pray about them or help in some other way. But He will not continue entrusting such confidences to those who repeat everything they hear.

Ministering Confidentially. Prophecy that must be delivered with specific private details should be ministered confidentially. This is especially important when ministering to church or national leaders in authority. Since a prophetic word to a leader will affect those under the leader, the leader should be allowed to consider the word in private and pray about its implementation before making it public. Nevertheless, these words should still be taped, and the recipient should still follow the proper steps in receiving and applying a personal prophecy.

This does not mean that every word given to a leader should be given privately, for we see many scriptural examples of prophets prophesying publicly to kings and leaders. In fact, public prophetic ministry is often given to affirm leaders in the eyes of the people and to consecrate them for leadership responsibilities. Aside from corrective words, the most common kind of prophetic word to a leader that should be given in private is one about a change in leadership.

The Examples of Jehu and Saul. For example, Elisha once instructed a young prophet to go to the general Jehu, anoint him king, and give him a personal prophecy—not in front of the other generals, but privately in an inner chamber. Then General Jehu himself went out and revealed, when the others asked, the word the prophet had spoken about the new change in leadership (2Kings 9:1-13). This incident sets an example for us: The prophet should give such a word to the leader and leave it to him or her to determine the time and place for implementing the word.

When Samuel pronounced judgment on Saul for his failure to obey God, and prophesied an eventual change of leadership for Israel, the prophet gave the personal prophecy in a private setting. We know the meeting was private because afterward, Saul asked Samuel to publicly worship with him so he would be honored before the elders (1Sam.15:13-31). Then Samuel went to Jesse's home and gave a personal prophecy to David in private, declaring that he would be the next king.

We have no indication that the nation of Israel ever knew the content of these prophecies during Saul's lifetime. If they had, they almost certainly would have plotted and taken action to make the prophecies come to pass. Some Israelites no doubt would have overthrown Saul by assassinating him, deposing him, or manipulating him out of power by prayer and prophesying.

Samuel's speaking this word privately may well have kept Saul from being immediately replaced by David. This was an important precaution since David was just a young boy at the time and was not ready yet to assume the throne. Wise and mature prophets today will imitate Samuel's example, practicing discretion in their delivery of such sensitive information.

Keep in mind that in this situation God was not attempting to hide Saul's sin. In fact, on a number of other occasions the Bible records that the Lord publicly exposed and judged leaders through prophetic words. But the private setting of Saul's word of judgment evidently served to accomplish God's perfect timing for raising young David up to rule in Saul's place.

Changes in Local Church Leadership. This insight should be kept in mind, for example, when a prophet is ministering in a local church and sees that the senior pastor is called to be an apostle with translocal ministry. God may even show the prophet who the next pastor will be from among those on staff or in leadership. It would probably be wisest in such a situation to share this in private with the senior pastor for his or her prayerful consideration. Otherwise, a public prophetic utterance on the matter could cause the congregation to be insecure or even divided on the status of the church leadership. A private word allows the senior pastor to decide if and when to share the prophecy publicly.

Divine wisdom and discretion are needed to minister prophetically in circumstances like these. For that reason, a prophet needs to be trained in matters of leadership and protocol.

18. SHOULD PROPHETIC UTTERANCES SERVE AS THE SOLE BASIS FOR DETERMINING DOCTRINE AND PRACTICE?

Church order, doctrine, and practices in New Testament times were not established solely by the prophecy, visions, dreams, or personal experiences of a private individual: "No prophecy of the scripture is of any private interpretation" (2Pet.1:20).

The clearest New Testament example of the correct process for establishing doctrine and practice is found in the book of Acts. There, Luke tells us about Peter's vision and experience concerning the Mosaic dietary and circumcision laws, and how these matters were judged by the Council at Jerusalem (see Acts chapters 10, 11 and 15).

Peter had a private revelation through a vision that the dietary laws, and the separation between Jew and Gentile they represented, were no longer to be followed. That revelation was then confirmed by a personal experience: He was led supernaturally to a place where Gentiles were meeting, preached the gospel to them, and witnessed the Holy Spirit save them and fill them before his very eyes—even though none of them had first become circumcised converts to Judaism.

A Church Council. When other believers challenged the notion that Gentiles could enter the Church without first undergoing circumcision and conversion to Judaism, the matter was brought before a council of the apostles and elders at Jerusalem, the mother church. There Peter gave his testimony of what had happened: a vision, an angelic visitation, and a sovereign move of God on the Gentiles. Paul and Barnabas added their testimony of how they had seen the Holy Spirit sovereignly bestowing on the Gentiles all the benefits of Christ apart from the Mosaic law.

The issue was debated and examined carefully in the light of the (Old Testament) scriptures. James, the overseer of the church, finally declared after the debate that "the words of the prophets are in agreement with this" (Ja.15:15)—that is, this new doctrine and practice was in keeping with the Scriptures. Then a written statement of their conclusion was published in the churches.

No Automatic Acceptance of Private Revelations. Despite Peter's high status in the early church as one of the Twelve who was closest to Jesus, the church did not automatically accept his private revelation and personal experience as a new standard for doctrine and practice. These supernatural experiences were eye-openers for the council and served as confirming evidence. But the issues still had to be submitted to the wisest leadership in the Church for discussion in the light of Scripture. Only when this special council determined that the new teaching was compatible with God's written revelation was it incorporated into the body of established doctrine for the New Testament church.

Today we should follow the New Testament example. Our doctrine and practice must not be established by private revelations or experiences either. To do so would be to invite error, cultism and eccentric ideas to flourish; that is how groups like the Mormons and Christian Scientists began.

19. WHAT ARE THE DIFFERENT LEVELS OF GIFT-INGS AND ANOINTINGS IN THE PROPHETIC REALM, AND ARE ALL WHO PROPHESY CON-SIDERED PROPHETS?

When Paul asked the Corinthians rhetorically, "Are all prophets?" (1Cor.12:28), the answer was clearly "NO!" Yet he also insisted in the same letter that we are all to covet to prophesy (14:39) and that we may all prophesy one by one (14:31).

All believers may flow in the spirit of prophecy which comes upon a congregation, or in the gift of prophecy, which is given to certain believers. But clearly, if all may prophesy and yet not all are prophets, then all who prophesy are not prophets. Even Saul, who was tormented by an evil spirit and was certainly not a prophet, nevertheless prophesied when he got around the prophets (1Sam.19:24).

Prophets Do Not Just Prophesy. Prophets are not just individuals that prophesy; they are one of the five-fold ministries of Christ who hold governmental authority in the Church. In fact, prophesying may make up only a small portion of some prophets' ministries. They may also be gifted to teach, shepherd or administrate.

Isaiah was a consultant to kings and governments. Joseph administered an international food distribution program. David ruled all of Israel, led armies and had an anointed music ministry. So the prophet's ministry obviously cannot be limited to just prophesying.

Levels of Authority. Even among the prophets there are differences in levels of authority. Those who have years of seasoned and proven ministries and who have been through God's process of testing and maturity will have more authoritative prophetic pronouncements than the "sons of the prophets" who are new in ministry.

Elijah, for example, moved in great authority by shutting up the heavens and calling down fire. Yet at the same time he ministered, there were at least a hundred other prophets whom Obadiah (Ahab's governor) had hidden in caves to protect them from Jezebel's wrath (1Kings 18:4). Samuel was a key prophetic leader in Israel's history whose words never fell to the ground (1Sam.3:19), and because of his stature and maturity he was the overseer of an entire company of prophets (19:20).

Today as well, God is raising up elders in the prophetic ministry who can be fathers and mothers to birth and train many in this restorational move of the Holy Spirit. These will be mature men and women in ministry who can help us avoid the excesses and imbalances of immature prophetic ministry. They will stress character as well as a gifting, and seeking God's face as well as His hand of favor.

17

PROPHETICALLY KNOWING
THE
TIMES, SEASONS AND END-TIME EVENTS

The Scripture tells us plainly that God has a calendar for planet earth. There are "times and seasons" in His purposes for the world—but His timing is not the same as ours. For that reason, the Church must learn to discern the times.

The prophets especially must be aware of God's timetable. Like the men of the ancient Hebrew tribe Issachar, who "understood the times and knew what Israel should do" (1Chr.12:32 NIV), we need divine insight into heaven's purposes for our generation. And we must understand where we are headed as we approach the end of the Church Age.

This isn't to say, of course, that we can know the exact date of Jesus' return. The Lord told His disciples: "No one knows about that day or hour, not even the angels in heaven, nor the Son, but only the Father" (Matt.24:36 NIV). Paul added this warning when he told the Thessalonians: "Now brothers, about times and dates, we do not need to write you, for you know very well that the day of the Lord will come like a thief in the night" (1Thess.5:1,2 NIV).

Nevertheless, Jesus also said that we would know the **season** of His coming, that we could tell when it was **near**, just as the signs of spring let us know that summer is near (see Luke 21:29-31). And Paul told the Thessalonians that even though they couldn't know the exact date of Jesus' return, they shouldn't be totally caught off guard by it: "But you, brothers, are not in darkness so that this day should surprise you like a thief" (1Thess.5:4 NIV).

I believe that the "summer" Jesus spoke of is near. To explain more clearly why I think that's the case, we must take a few minutes to outline an overview of God's times and seasons throughout church history.

An Overview. Church historians have many ways of dividing up the period of God's dealings with His people. Dispensationalists often speak of seven ages or dispensations, beginning with Adam. Covenant theologians usually mark time by various covenants between God and His people.

Through my own study of church history, I've concluded that God seems to do something different with His people every 2,000 years, and every 500 years as well. If you allow for a variance of ten to forty years on either side of some rounded dates (again, we don't know the exact times of God's timetable), a pattern emerges.

Every 2,000 years, for example, God creates a new race. In the year "0" He made the human race when He made Adam. Two thousand years later he called Abraham to found the Hebrew race. Another 2,000 years later He sent Jesus to establish the Church race.

Now, yet another 2,000 years later, the Church race is soon to become the Kingdom race—a race with immortal bodies as well as immortal spirits. Through the resurrection/translation event promised in Scripture (see 1Cor.15:51-54; 1Thess.4:15-18), we will receive renewed, glorified bodies to serve in the kingdom of God on earth.

Five-Hundred Year Periods. Consider as well the 500-year increments of God's calendar. Five centuries after Jesus established the Church, it fell into a period of deterioration. Another five hundred years later—A.D. 1000—was the "midnight" of those Dark Ages. Soon after the year A.D. 1500 the great restoration of the Church began with Martin Luther, the Protestant reformer.

Now, I believe, sometime not long after the year A.D. 2000, we will see the restoration of the Church completed. Already God has been restoring to His Church in our generation the apostles, prophets, evangelists, pastors and teachers. According to Scripture, these five-fold ministries are needed "for the perfecting of the saints, for the work of the ministry, for the edifying of the Body of Christ, till we all come in the unity of the faith, and of the knowledge of the Son of God, unto a perfect man, unto the measure of the stature of the fullness of Christ" (Eph.4:12,13).

The Bible says that Jesus is being held in the heavens until the time of the restoration of all things (see Acts 3:21). So when the restoration of the Church is complete, I expect to see Jesus return.

The Role of the Prophetic Movement. Each major event in the history of God's people is accompanied by activity in heaven. When Jesus was born, the angels came down from heaven rejoicing and praising God. When He died and rose again from the grave, I'm sure heaven was celebrating. And now, as the Church's restoration moves toward completion, I believe that a number of activities are taking place in heaven.

The Prophetic Movement plays a key role in this process. I believe that the prophets will take what has been divinely decreed in heaven and release it within the Church on earth so that God's people can be activated to minister His purposes in the world.

What Has This Movement Released in Heaven and Activated On Earth? The Company of Prophets now appearing has the same "Elijah spirit" John the Baptist had, so I believe that what happened in John's day is also happening now.

The Old Testament prophet Malachi prophesied that Elijah would come "before the great and terrible day of the Lord" (Mal.4:5). In referring to this scripture, Jesus said: " 'To be sure, Elijah comes and will restore all things. But I tell you, Elijah has already come, and they did not recognize him....' Then the disciples understood that He was talking to them about John the Baptist" (Matt.17:11-13 NIV).

John came "before the Lord in the spirit and power of Elijah...to make ready a people prepared for the Lord" (Luke 1:17 NIV). He was a single prophet who prepared for the personal coming of Jesus the Messiah. Today, an entire Company of Prophets are going before the Lord in the spirit and power of Elijah, and they will prepare the way for His second coming. So there are a number of parallels between John's appearing and the appearing of the prophets today.

Activation. First of all, John's prophetic ministry released the time for Jesus to be activated and manifested as the Messiah, with mighty demonstrations of the Holy Spirit's power. In a similar way, the Company of Prophets today is preparing a way and making ready a people for the Lord's coming. The Company of Prophets activated during the Prophetic Movement are releasing the Church in mighty demonstrations of supernatural utterances and miracles.

No doubt all heaven got excited when John began to come forth as a prophet and his ministry was manifested, because it meant that Jesus' time was at hand. Today, Jesus is the One who's celebrating. The activation of the Prophetic Movement indicates that a way is being prepared for Him to return to His beloved Bride, the Church—so you can imagine how glad He is to see the prophets come forth. Just put yourself in His situation: If you really wanted to go somewhere to see someone special, but it was up to a particular group of people to prepare the way for you, think how excited you'd get when you saw that those people were finally getting activated to accomplish their purpose!

Transition. John's ministry was significant in a second way as well. He signified a time of transition for God's people. John was a sign that the dispensation of the law was closing and the Church was emerging. In a similar way, the present-day company of the prophets is signifying that the mortal Church Age of mercy and grace is coming to a close and the day of judgment is beginning—a transition that will take place in a single generation, just as the transition did in John's time.

The Transition Generation Is Alive. A third characteristic of John's ministry was that it declared that the generation alive on earth at that time would see and experience the transition from the age of law to the Church Age (see Matt.24:34). So I believe that the appearance of the Company of Prophets today means that a generation alive today on planet earth will see the transition from the Church Age to the Kingdom Age.

I don't know whether it will be my generation, my son's generation, or my grandchildren's generation. But I believe that some of us alive today could be here when, as the apostle Paul said, "we will be changed" and go right on into eternity.

The Seventh Trumpet. When the apostle John was given a look into heaven and into the future, he recorded that he saw seven angels with trumpets. Each time one of those angels in heaven blew a trumpet, something happened on earth. John wrote:

> But in the days of the voice of the seventh angel, when he shall begin to sound, the mystery of God should be finished, as he hath declared to his servants the prophets....And the seventh angel sounded; and there were great voices in heaven, saying, The kingdoms of

this world are become the kingdoms of our Lord, and of His Christ; and He shall reign for ever and ever (Rev.10:7; 11:15).

I believe that God has apostles and prophets to echo on earth in human terminology what has been sounded in heaven by the angels. What was decreed and released in heaven is decreed and released through the prophets and apostles on earth. What was bound or loosed in heaven by the angels is bound or loosed on earth by the prophets and apostles.

We should note here that we can preach, teach and prophesy a message on earth all we like, but until it is decreed in heaven and the trumpet is sounded, it won't work—just like you can't make your own personal prophecy work until it's God's time for that to happen. We can only prophetically decree on earth what has already been decreed by the angels and by God's divine decree in heaven. In the same way, we can't just bind anything on earth on our own whim and desire; we can only bind what has already been bound in heaven.

We read that John was speaking here, not of the resurrection/translation—the "twinkling of an eye"—but of a period of time: "in the **days** of the voice of the seventh angel when he shall **begin** to sound…" (v. 7). There is no indication how long the angel sounds. But as he **begins** to sound, the Prophetic Movement takes place on planet earth. Then the mysteries of God, the fullness of truth and life and understanding, are unveiled as Jesus comes forth in the Church as the way, the truth and the life.

John says the angel keeps sounding, and that tells us that the prophets' voice will never die out again. The voices will keep declaring God's Word until every mystery is revealed, every truth fulfilled, every scripture worked out—until God's way is prepared and His people are ready for the coming the Lord. When the prophets finish sounding, great voices in heaven declare that the kingdom's of this world have become the kingdoms of our Lord (see Rev.11:15).

The Prophetic Movement Will Not Diminish. What God has begun with this great Prophetic Movement is not just a little thing hidden in a corner. It's global, universal, for it is happening in every nation. It's not just something to add a new little dimension to the Church. It's a divine decree, a divine destiny, a move of God that's affecting heaven and earth.

The Prophetic Movement is getting Jesus excited because He knows that the Father has released the seventh angel to begin sounding his trumpet in heaven, and His great Company of Prophets have been activated into their prophetic ministry on Earth. Heaven knows this is the hour; we need to know it as well. In this day, God's consummation of the ages is at hand. The prophets have arisen and been restored to the Church, and they will not cease prophesying until the kingdoms of the earth become the kingdoms of God and His anointed Church.

That means the Prophetic Movement will not "phase out" or diminish. Instead, it will grow and grow, and when the apostolic movement is born, we will walk side by side. Apostles, prophets and prophetic worshippers will flow together, and the evangelists, pastors and teachers who have the present truth will flow along as well.

The Greatest Sign. Judging from Old Testament prophecy, what was the greatest sign on earth two thousand years ago that the Messiah was about to be manifested? It was John the Baptist, the Elijah prophet (see Mal.4:5). So what is the greatest sign in this century of how close we are to the coming of the Lord again? In the first half of the 20th century it was the restoration of the nation of Israel in 1948. But the greatest sign we have in the last half of the 20th century is the restoration of the prophets. The Prophetic Movement was birthed in the Church in 1988. (See page 96 of *Prophets and the Prophetic Movement* for more details).

Consider: we are living in days that are just as momentous as those when John the Baptist appeared to prepare the way for

Jesus to be manifested as the Messiah. God's great prophetic company will be manifesting the kingdom of God, because the gospel (demonstration) of the Kingdom must go into all the world for a witness before the end comes (see Matt.24:14).

God will give every nation a witness that Jesus is greater than Mohammed or Buddha, greater than all the other gods, false religions and systems of this world. We will demonstrate that Jesus knows more and can do more than any other god. And the prophets and apostles will be instrumental in raising up the most radical, devil-hating, God-loving people that have ever lived since Joshua took a new generation into Canaan.

Crossing the Jordan. There is yet another parallel between the ministry of John the Baptist and the current Prophetic Movement: John prepared the people for Jesus and the Church Age by baptizing them in the Jordan River. The Prophetic Movement has "opened up" the Church's spiritual Jordan in the sense that it has opened a way to cross over and enter our "promised land" to possess it.

Day of Judgment. What else has happened since the Prophetic Movement has come forth? The day of judgment and righteousness has come to the Church. The Bible says that "judgment must begin at the house of God" (1Pet.4:17). In the decade of the eighties, when the prophets came forth, judgment did indeed begin with the house of God.

Since 1988, when the Prophetic Movement was birthed, sins have been exposed nationally—political leaders, financial leaders and spiritual leaders as well. Just look at how many folks were publicly uncovered in the media after 1988.

Look as well at what happened on the international scene. According to God's commission to Jeremiah, the prophetic ministry is to root out, tear down, build up and plant (Jer.1:10). Since 1988, the Iron Curtain has been ripped apart and the Berlin Wall has been pulled down. And I've heard that there were a number of prophets in the formerly Communist nations that had been prophesying those judgments.

What has been done in secret is being shouted from the housetops. We can no longer get away with what we used to get away with in past movements. God is saying, "I won't put up with wrong financial dealings. I won't tolerate sexual immorality. I won't let you pamper the flesh." In the past God may have overlooked our ignorance, but now He commands us to repent (see Acts 17:30).

The Ax at the Root. John the Baptist declared: "The ax is already at the root of the trees, and every tree that does not produce good fruit will be cut down and thrown into the fire" (Matt.3:10 NIV). The same is true today as the Company of Prophets comes forth.

The Holiness Movement that spread across the Church in the nineteenth century was ordained of God to wholly sanctify the Church from worldliness and carnal activities. God was seeking to do an inward work that would be manifested by holy living. But the preachers in the movement began to preach more on the outward human works than the transformation of the inner man. When they talked about holiness, what they usually meant was a form of anti-worldliness, or what I refer to as "clothesline holiness." They focused on lots of "don'ts" : Don't wear that. Don't do that. Don't go here. Don't go there. They got away from the real issues of heart and life and spirit.

As a result, the Holiness Movement simply "pruned" back the individual sins that it focused on. But the ax wasn't laid to the root. The root is the motive of the heart, and our sinful motives must be dealt with if we're to be truly cleansed and wholly sanctified.

The Company of the Prophets has arisen with an ax in their hand. Today that ax is being laid to the very root motivations of every child of God who is serious about going on with Jesus Christ.

No More Indulgence. Back in the days of the deliverance and healing evangelism movement, and even in the Charismatic Movement, some people would get up and preach, pray, heal the sick, even cast out demons—and then they would go back to their hotel room to commit adultery. Others would get drunk before they went up on the platform, and when they staggered around, people thought they were staggering under the power of God.

That day has ceased. God has said that from this day forward, the prophets are to root out, tear down and expose everything. So it's time to pray through and get the victory over that weakness God calls sin, rebellion and self-will.

The Scripture tells us we must "cleanse ourselves from all filthiness of the flesh and spirit, perfecting holiness in the fear of God" (2Cor.7:1). Sadly enough, sometimes we ask God to do things that He tells us to do ourselves. But cleansing ourselves in this way is something we must do.

No doubt we can't fight the flesh with the flesh. We can only put to death the deeds of the flesh by the Spirit, through spiritual power and spiritual grace. But it's within our power to rise up and take dominion over the flesh (Rom.6:6-14; 8:12,13).

We can't be instruments of judgment until we ourselves have been judged. We can't be purgers until we ourselves have been purged. Judgment through the Prophetic Movement in the house of God has first begun with prophetic people themselves.

In fact, God won't place anyone in the judgment ministry who hasn't first been purged of all desire to pronounce judgment. Those who have a zeal to straighten everyone up and wipe everyone out have the wrong spirit. They need to be sanctified in the love of God.

Even so, God's love is not like we often imagine it to be. He's not a pampering, permissive, flesh-pleasing, Santa Claus. God's love is tough. In fact, His love put Jesus on the cross.

Since the Father let Jesus suffer all that He did—humiliation, thirty-nine stripes, thorns on His head, nails in His hands and feet, hung naked on the cross—just so that He could **purchase** the Church, what will God put you and me through to **perfect** the Church? If we're not walking in holiness, God will crucify us to perfect His Church just as He crucified Jesus to purchase His Church.

Prophets Are Refiners. Through the Prophet Malachi, God said: "See, I will send my messenger, who will prepare the way before me. Then suddenly the Lord you are seeking will come to His temple; the messenger of the covenant, whom you desire, will come" (Mal.3:1 NIV).

When God speaks of His messengers, he usually refers to His prophets. So I believe He's saying here that He will send His Company of Prophets, and they will prepare His way before Him. The Lord shall suddenly come to His temple—the Church—with a prophetic voice. And that is happening today.

Malachi's prophecy goes on:

> But who can endure the day of His coming? Who can stand when He appears? For He will be like a refiner's fire or a launderer's soap. He will sit as a refiner and a purifier…. (Mal.3:2,3 NIV).

Jesus has set the true prophets in His Church as refiners and purifiers of His people so they, as Malachi says, can "bring offerings in righteousness…acceptable to the Lord" (v. 3).

I believe in the literal, physical coming of Jesus to the earth. But leading up to that time, I also believe, Jesus has come to His people a number of times, each time in a new dimension. He came in the Protestant Movement, in the Holiness Movement, in the Pentecostal Movement, in the Charismatic Movement. He came to bring truth and reality, life and ministry. Now He has come in the Prophetic Movement, bringing the refiner's fire to purify the Church.

God's Plumb Line. God told Isaiah that He would make "righteousness the plumb line" (Is.28:17 NIV). The plumb line is what a carpenter uses to make sure the whole building is properly aligned with the cornerstone. So one Bible translation says that God would have His people be "rigidly righteous." And it is the prophets who are to bring righteousness in the Church: right attitudes, a right spirit, right motives, right actions, right relationships.

Why did God anoint Jesus above all others? Hebrews tells us it was because He loved righteousness and hated wickedness (see Heb.1:9). Jesus had a divinely perfect love for righteousness and a divinely perfect hatred of iniquity. He shared God's hatred of everything that was not in keeping with the character of heaven.

A number of Bible passages tell us that we too are to hate evil and love good (see for example Ps. 97:10, Amos 5:15). We are to love people yet hate their sin (see Jude 1:23). In doing so, we become more like Jesus and reflect the character of God Himself.

Past movements in the Church have tended to focus on the love of God and the goodness of God, which were a necessary corrective to some faulty images of Him that the Church had come to have. But now the Prophetic Movement is revealing the severity of God as well. We are reminding the Church that "our God is a consuming fire" (Heb.12:29 NIV). The Church must behold not only the goodness of God but also His severity. (Rom.11:22)

A Stricter Measure. I believe that God is more strict and exacting in His demands at the beginning of a divinely inspired movement in order to set His standard. We can see this reality illustrated in several biblical events.

We all know the Old Testament story of Achan, one of the Israelites who accompanied Joshua into Canaan (see Joshua 7). When Achan disobeyed God and took some of the plunder for himself, he was severely judged. In obedience to God Israel stoned and burned him, his family and all his belongings.

Why was God so exacting in His standard for Achan and the other Israelites at that time? God expected them to be rigidly righteous because they had just entered Canaan—a new era, a new dimension, a new ministry for God's people. They had just established new truth and a new way of life, so God said, in effect, "When I tell you to do something, do exactly what I tell you. Don't interpret it and apply it according to your own understanding." This is the same standard that God required of Moses when He commanded him to make the Tabernacle exactly according to the pattern given on Mt. Sinai.

Achan's main sin wasn't stealing. His root sin and character flaw was that he took what had been designated for God and put it in his own tent. Many today are doing the same, and God is saying that He won't tolerate it any more.

The same was true for Saul. As the first king of Israel, he was inaugurating a new era in the history of God's people. So when Saul disobeyed and misinterpreted the prophecies that Prophet Samuel had given him and acted selfishly by sparing the best of the enemy's flocks and herds, God judged him severely. He canceled Saul's prophecies and his ministry. He tore the kingdom away from Saul and gave it to David and David's descendants instead (see 1Sam.15).

Ananias and Sapphira. In the book of Acts we read about how the new covenant was established. The New Testament Church was being instituted and established. No wonder, then, that when Ananias and Sapphira lied to the apostle Peter about what they had done with their finances, God judged them severely (see Acts 5:1-11). Peter issued God's prophetic death penalty, and it came to pass immediately.

On the other hand, consider Barnabas, who sold his property and laid all the proceeds at the feet of the apostles. He acted with integrity, doing what Ananias and Sapphira had only claimed to do. This same Barnabas went on to be a co-laborer with Paul and one of the great apostles of the New Testament.

God was holding His people to a strict measure. Financial integrity led Barnabas to promotion and a fruitful ministry. But financial selfishness and greed led Ananias and Sapphira to death. How the people handled their finances determined whether their ministry would be established, grow and experience promotion, or whether it would wither and die.

Godly Fear Followed by Miracles. The result was that "great fear seized the whole church and all who heard about these events" (Acts 5:11 NIV). I think the same thing will begin happening today. God is restoring back to the Church a sense of the reverential fear of the Lord.

That fear of God was itself followed by "many miraculous signs and wonders among the people" performed by the apostles (Acts 5:12 NIV). Again, I expect that to happen in our own day as well. When the fear of God comes on His Church, resulting in righteousness, then many signs and wonders will be wrought by the prophets and apostles.

God's Last Day Call. Today God is calling not only the Prophetic movement but the whole Church to a rigid standard of personal righteousness and ministerial ethics. As prophetic ministers in this generation we will be called on to purify and refine the people of God, but we must first be purified and refined ourselves. God grant us grace to learn how to hate evil and love righteousness just as He does—so that we can avoid all the pitfalls and speak the pure word of God to the Church and the world.

EXPLANATION AND DEFINITIONS
OF
PRESENT TRUTH PROPHETIC TERMS

FIVE-FOLD MINISTRY

These are the five-fold ascension gift ministers as revealed in Eph.4:11—Apostle, Prophet, Evangelist, Pastor and Teacher. They are not gifts of the Holy Spirit per se, but an extension of Christ's headship ministry to the Church. Their primary ministry and function is to teach, train, activate and mature the saints for the work of their ministries.

APOSTLE

One of the five-fold ministries of Eph.4:11, The Apostle is a foundation laying ministry (Eph.2:20) which is seen in the N.T. establishing new churches (Paul's missionary Journeys), correcting error by establishing proper order and structure (First Epistle to the Corinthians), and acting as an oversight ministry which fathers other ministries (1Cor.4:15, 2Cor.11:28). The N.T. Apostle has a revelatory anointing (Eph.3:5), and frequently demonstrates signs, wonders and miracles. More will be known and manifested concerning the apostle during the next restorational movement.

PROPHET

A man of God whom Christ has given the ascension gift of a "prophet." (Eph.4:11, 1Cor.12:28; 1Cor.14:29; Acts 11:27; Acts 13:1.) A prophet is one of the five-fold ascension gift ministers who are an extension of Christ's ministry to the Church. An anointed minister who has the gifted ability to perceive and speak the specific mind of Christ to individuals, churches, businesses and nations.

GREEK: "prophetes" (prof-ay-tace) a foreteller, an inspired speaker. (STRONG'S Concordance, Pg. 62; VINES Concordance Pg. 894) A proclaimer of a divine message, denoted among the Greeks as an interpreter of the oracles of gods. In the Septuagint it is the translation of the word "roeh"—a seer—indicating that the prophet was one who had immediate intercourse with God

(1Sam.9:9). It also translates the word "nabhi," meaning either "one in whom the message from God springs forth, or one to whom anything is secretly communicated." (Amos 3:7; Eph.3:5)

PROPHETESS *GREEK:*

"prophetis"—the feminine of prophet (Gr. prophetes). A woman of God who has been given the divine prophetic ability to perceive and speak the mind of Christ on specific matters to particular people. STRONGS: a "female foreteller or an inspired woman." A specially called woman who functions like the New Testament prophet to minister to the Body of Christ with inspired speaking and prophetic utterance (Acts 2:17; 21:9; Luke 2:36; Isa.8:3; 2Chron.34:22; Jude 4:4; Ex.15:20). Prophetess is the proper title for a woman with this ascension gift and calling. Prophet is the proper title for a man with this ascension gift and calling.

EVANGELIST

The traditional view of the evangelist is a bearer of the "Good News", proclaiming the gospel to the unbelieving world. This is exemplified by modern day evangelists who preach the message of salvation in crusades and the like. However, Phillip, the N.T. Evangelists mentioned in Acts 21:8 demonstrated a strong supernatural dimension to the Evangelistic ministry. Philip preached the gospel to the lost (Acts 8:5), moved in miracles (8:6), delivered people from demons (8:7), received instructions from an Angel (8:26), had revelation knowledge (8:29), and was supernaturally translated from Gaza to Azotus (8:26,40). We are looking forward to the restoration of this type of Prophetic Evangelist to the Body of Christ.

PASTOR

"Poiment," a shepherd, one who tends herds or flocks (not merely one who feeds them), is used metaphorically of Christian pastors. "Episkopeo" (overseer, bishop) is an overseer, and "Pesbuteros" (elder) is another term for the same person as bishop or overseer. (Vine's). The title normally given to the senior minister of the local church, regardless of his five-fold calling. A shepherding ministry to feed and care for the flock. Responsibilities that appear connected with pastoral ministry include oversight and care of the saints, providing spiritual food for their growth and development,

leadership, guidance and counsel. Prophetic pastors not only do the things normally associated with pastoring, but also move in supernatural graces and giftings of God (prophesying, word of knowledge, healing) and have the vision and willingness to develop the saints in their gifts and callings.

TEACHER

An instructor of truth. (2Tim.3:16) All scripture is given by inspiration of God, and is profitable for doctrine, for reproof, for correction, for instruction in righteousness. New Testament Prophetic Teacher is one who not only teaches the letter of the word, but ministers with divine life and Holy Spirit anointing (2Cor.3:6). He exhibits keen spiritual insight and discernment into the Word of God and its personal application to believers.

PROPHETIC MINISTERS

Prophetic ministers are all other ministers who do not have the office of the "prophet" but who do hold another office of the five-fold ministry and believe that there are prophets in the Church today. They may move in prophetic ministry by prophesying with the gift of prophecy, or by giving personal prophecy with a prophetic presbytery, do prophetic counseling and ministry with gifts of the Holy Spirit, or minister in prophetic worship. All five-fold New Testament ministers in whichever office should be able to speak a rhema word revealing the mind and purpose of God for specific situations and people (2Cor.3:6; 1Cor.14:31).

PROPHETIC PEÓPLE

They are the people of God who are full of the Holy Spirit and are fulfilling the scriptural command to "desire spiritual gifts, covet to prophesy" (1Cor.12:39; 14:1,2,39). They believe in, propagate and support the ministry of apostles and prophets in the church today. They are earnestly desiring gifts and are exercising their spiritual senses in order to be fully educated and activated in all the gifts of the Holy Spirit which Christ has ordained for them, including but not limited to the gift of prophecy (Heb.5:14; 1Cor.12: 1,7,11).

PROPHETIC MINISTRY

This includes all the ways and means by which the Holy Spirit makes known the heart and mind of Christ to mankind. Prophetic ministry includes the ministry of the prophet, prophetic ministers, and all prophetic people. It includes all the ministry and manifestations of the Holy Spirit and all the scriptural ways in which God can be praised. This includes prophetic worship with singing, praising, prophesying, song of the Lord, praise-dance, mime, and sign language. In fact, it includes all dedicated physical expressions which may properly glorify God and edify the Church.

PROPHETIC ANOINTING AND MANTLE

An in-depth study of the word "anoint" reveals that it was used to consecrate people to a particular position or ministry. In ministering with prophetic anointing, it means you are enduing people with the presence of Christ and the gifts and graces of the Holy Spirit. Is.10:27 declares yokes are destroyed because of the anointing. In present day application this means the manifest presence of God to meet specific needs.

To say a person has a prophetic anointing means that they have the calling to move in the prophetic ministry. It does not necessarily mean this person has the calling of the office of "prophet." Prophetic mantle has a similar meaning. If someone has prophesied you have a prophetic mantle, it implies that you have the gifted ability to minister in prophetic ministry, to what realm will be determined by time and use. (Ex.28:41; Psalms 2:2; 23:5; 105:15; Zec.4:6; Heb.1:19).

PROPHECY

GREEK: "propheteia," a noun which "signifies the speaking forth of the mind and counsel of God. It is the declaration of that which cannot be known by natural means. It is the forth-telling of the will of God, whether with reference to the past, the present, or the future." (VINES, p.893). New Testament prophecy functions in three realms:

1. Jesus giving inspired testimony and praise through one of his saints by **prophetic utterance or song of the Lord**. (Heb.2:12; Rev.19:10.)

2. One of the manifestations of the Holy Spirit called the **gift of prophecy** which brings edification, exhortation and comfort to the Body of Christ. (1Cor.12:10; Rom.12:6)

3. *The prophet speaking by **divine utterance** the mind and coun-sels of God and giving a **rhema** word for edification, direc-tion, correction, confirmation, and instruction in righteousness. (1Cor.14:29; 2Tim.3:16,17)*

A truly, divinely inspired prophecy is the Holy Spirit expressing the thoughts and desires of Christ through a human voice.

PROPHETIC PRESBYTERY

Prophetic Presbytery is when two or more prophets and/or prophetic ministers lay hands on and prophesy over individuals at a specified time and place. Prophetic presbyteries are conducted for several reasons:

1. *For revealing a church member's membership ministry in the Body of Christ.*
2. *For ministering a prophetic **rhema** word of God to in-dividuals.*
3. *For impartation and activation of divinely ordained gifts, graces and callings.*
4. *For the revelation, clarification and confirmation of leader-ship ministry in the local church.*
5. *For the "laying on of hands and prophecy" over those called and properly prepared to be a five-fold minister.*

PROPHETIC PRAYING

Basically it is Spirit-directed praying. Praying with natural un-derstanding is asking God's help about matters of which we have natural knowledge. Prophetic praying is prophesying with prayer phraseology. It is praying out of one's spirit in his natural known tongue, flowing the same as one praying out of his spirit in un-known tongues. The prayer is on target and touches specific areas unknown in the natural to the one praying and uses prophetic motivation, word of knowledge, discerning of spirits, word of wis-dom, etc. Intercessory prayer is much more effective when it moves into the realm of prophetic praying. In ministering to people in churches who do not understand or promote prophesy-ing, prophetic ministry can still bless the people through prophetic praying. Instead of prophesying, "thus sayeth the Lord" or "the Lord shows me that..." you verbalize by saying, "Lord, we pray for this"…. *"Jesus, you see what he, she have been going through regarding….or how difficult it has been in the area of…or overcoming…. etc. "*

PROPHETIC COUNSELING

Prophetic counseling serves a little different purpose than the ministry of the prophet, prophetic presbytery or general counseling. It is one-on-one ministry to help people with scriptural wisdom and insight, but also with the gifts of the Holy Spirit to discover root problems and minister deliverance, inner healing, etc. The word of knowledge and discerning of spirits are two key gifts necessary to move in this realm effectively. It allows the counselor to cut through hours of discussion and look beyond the veil of human reasoning to get right to the heart of the matter and bring resolution. This is what makes biblical counseling much more effective than the psychologist and psychiatrist who uses only human wisdom and psychology.

LOGOS

GREEK: "word"—the unchanging, inerrant, creative and inspired word of God. (See Ps.119:89 "Forever, O Lord, thy word (logos) is settled in heaven.") (See also 2Tim.3:16; 1 Cor.2:13) Logos is the entire written Word of God—the Bible. It is the complete revelation of God—His personage, character, plan and eternal purpose—as found in the Scripture.

RHEMA

GREEK: "word"—derived from the verb "to speak." (See Rom.10:17—"Faith cometh by hearing, and hearing by the word (rhema) of God.") A rhema is a word or an illustration God speaks directly to us, and it addresses our personal, particular situation. It is a timely, Holy Spirit-inspired Word from the logos that brings life, power and faith to perform and fulfill it. Its significance is exemplified in the injunction to take the "sword of the Spirit, which is the word (rhema) of God (Eph.6:17). It can be received through others such as by a prophetic word, or be an illumination given to one directly in their personal meditation time in the Bible or in prayer.

The logos is the fixed word of God—the Scriptures—and the rhema is a particular portion in line with the logos brought forth by the Spirit to be applied directly to something in our personal experience.

PROPHETIC WARFARE PRAISE AND WORSHIP

They are biblical expressions of praise and adoration (singing, clapping, dancing, lifting of hands, bowing, etc.) that are directed to God, inspired and directed by the Holy Spirit, and which come forth from the heart of man. Prophetic worship is where God's voice is heard and His presence felt as Christ begins to sing and express praise to the Father through His people. (Heb.2:12. Ps.22:22; Rev.19:10) These high praises of God both exalt the Lord and accomplish spiritual warfare in the heavenlies (Ps.149: 6-9; Eph.6:12; 2Cor.10:4-6). It is worship that is expressed in obedience to a prompting of God that brings forth a prophetic word, mantle or anointing that results in the manifestation of God's power (2Chron.20:14-22; 2Kings 3:15; 1Sam.10:5,6).

PROPHETIC SONG

A song that is inspired, anointed and directed by the Holy Spirit through an individual; usually spontaneous in nature, which expresses the mind of God in musical form. It is literally prophecy through song (referred to in the New Testament as spiritual songs) (See Col.3:16; Eph.5:19). These songs are directed to man for the purpose of edification, exhortation and comfort or may be directed to God as the Holy Spirit helps us express our deep devotion that we could not ordinarily express by ourselves (Heb.2:12; Rom.8:27; Zep.3:17—"The Lord thy God...will joy over you or through you with singing. ").

PROPHETIC PRAISE—DANCE AND SIGN

Physical movements that are inspirational and anointed by the Holy Spirit and many times accompanied by prophetic song (song of the Lord; spiritual songs.) (See Ex.15:20-21; 1Sam.21:11). It is used in praise, adoration and worship to God which can in itself bring in the prophetic mantle (1Sam.18:6). It may be spontaneous or choreographed (preplanned). At times, it may communicate divine thoughts, ideas and purposes—a visible expression of what God is saying (Acts 21:10-11; Jb.42:5— "My ears have heard you, but now my eyes have seen you! ").

GRACE

Grace is God's divine unmerited enablements. It is God's free abilities (gifts, talents, etc.) being demonstrated through a human vessel in spite of sin and human frailties. It is having God's unearned supernatural ability to perform and execute what ever He has willed to the individual saint (Eph.2:8,9).

ACTIVATION

To challenge God's people with the truth to receive and manifest the grace to do what the Bible says they can do. It is arousing, triggering, stirring, and releasing God's abilities within the saints. Gifts are given by the Holy Spirit but activated by the faith of the believer. Like the gift of Eternal Life, which is freely given, but is not activated within the individual until he believes in his heart and confesses with his mouth the Lord Jesus.

MEMBERSHIP MINISTRY

It is the individual members in the Body of Christ finding and manifesting their God given talents, abilities and callings, so that "every joint" will supply according to God's plans and purposes (Eph.4:16; 1Cor.12:7-11; 1Pet.4:10; 1Cor.14:26). Every member in the Body of Christ has a ministry and needs to be educated and activated into it.

SCHOOL OF THE HOLY SPIRIT

It is a training time in which God's saints are discipled in a "hot house" environment to discern the language of the Holy Spirit and manifest the gifts of the Holy Spirit under proper oversight and care. It is a time and place to learn to discern between the human soul and the realm of the Holy Spirit (Heb.5:14). It is a place where the saints allow the Holy Spirit and Word to operate in them, thereby causing them to exercise their spiritual senses (E.S.S.) and exercise their spiritual gifts (E.S.G.).

SHARING THE MIND OF CHRIST (Thought From The Throne):

It is the ability of every believer to draw upon the indwelling Christ and then sharing without using God-head terminology ("Thus saith the Lord, God says, or Thus saith Jesus," etc.), what he/she senses that Jesus, the Head, is saying to His Body. This is based upon 1Cor.2:16 and Rev.19:10.

COMPANY OF PROPHETS

This term today refers to the multitude of prophets God is raising up around the world in these last days to usher in the second coming of Jesus Christ. These prophets are being brought forth to be taught, trained and activated into their preordained ministry of "preparing the way for Jesus to return and establish His Kingdom over all the earth," (Is.40:3,5) as well as "making ready a people for Christ's return." They labor to purify the Church in righteousness and mature the saints for ministry, bridehood, co-laborship and co-reigning over God's vast domain (Lk.1:17; Eph.4:11; Eph.5:27).

SCHOOL OF PROPHETS (Sons of the Prophets)

Webster Dictionary: "Among the ancient Israelites, a school or college in which young men were educated and trained to become teachers of religion among the people. These students were called 'Sons of the Prophets'."

This refers to a group of people who have the calling to prophetic ministry and have come together at one place to be schooled in hearing and recognizing the true voice of God and how to properly and timely minister that word with grace and wisdom for the greatest glory to God and good to mankind. Samuel is recognized as founder of the School of Prophets which was continued by such prophets as Elijah and Elisha.

Based on 1Sam.19:20 regarding Saul, David and Samuel, the "school of the prophets" also serves as a covering for the Davidic company (the new order for ministry which God is raising up) to nurture and protect them from persecution of the old religious order (Saul's).

PROPHETS SEMINAR

These are seminars conducted through CI-NPM's home office in the panhandle of Florida to teach, train and activate saints concerning the gifts of the spirit and prophetic ministry in order to raise up a prophetic people of the Lord. Our ministry emphasis is to help instruct and activate prophets into a powerful, proper and pure function in the Body through impartation of gifts, prophetic presbytery, anointed teaching and practical participation in training. There is helpful instruction for pastors and other five-fold ministers to enhance their functioning and relationship with the prophetic ministry. Also, all in attendance receive a time of personal prophetic presbytery.

PROPHETS CONFERENCES

CI-NPM uses the word "conferences" when referring to meetings held in a local church which are sponsored by the local pastor. The prophets and other prophetic ministers speak and minister, but each message delivered does not necessarily deal with the prophetic. Also, due to the nature of the format, it is not possible to assure every person attending will personally receive prophetic ministry or presbytery with the laying on of hands.

REGIONAL PROPHETS CONFERENCES

These are CI-NPM sponsored prophets conferences held in different regions of the country in order to promote and propagate prophetic ministry in that area and to minister to a greater number of saints.

INTERNATIONAL PROPHETS CONFERENCES

International Prophets Conferences are a gathering of prophets, prophetic ministers and prophetic people from around the world. Christian International sponsored the first such conference known in the annals of Church history in the fall of 1987. The events are designed as a vehicle for assisting in disseminating prophetic ministry around the world that millions might be blessed and that a current consensus of what Christ is speaking to His Church may be attained and acted upon. Christian International and the Network of Prophetic Ministries plan an International Prophets Conference to be conducted in October every year to bring maturity, unity and fruit to the work of restoration that God is doing in the earth.

NETWORK OF PROPHETIC MINISTRIES (NPM)

A network of prophets, prophetic ministers and prophetic churches working and relating together under the covering of a proven governing board of apostles and prophets and an anointed senior prophet in order to produce mature and integrated prophetic ministry. An association and fellowship of those who have a heart and vision to see the prophetic ministry restored to full recognition and function in the Body of Christ along with those who feel a call to full time prophetic ministry. The Network of Prophetic Ministries provides a focal rallying point for prophetic ministers to have fellowship, instruction and an unifying force in order to be a clear voice of the Lord to the Church and the world.

PROPHETIC CHURCHES

This is the term used to identify the local churches within the Network of Prophetic Ministries and Churches. The word "churches" was not included in the term NPM because "ministries" covers both the prophetic minister and his church ministry. Those who qualify for recognition and promotion as a prophetic local church will have developed the following ministries within the church: qualified prophetic ministers and saints capable of forming prophetic presbytery; prophetic teams for healing, prophetic counseling, prophesying and ministering God's grace and deliverance by the gifts of the Holy Spirit. The prophetic pastor needs sufficient experience and maturity to give proper oversight, structure, motivation and direction in order to maintain control without restricting the flow of the prophetic ministry.

PROPHETIC LIFESTYLE

These are the people who live their lives according to the logos and rhema word of God. The logos is their general standard for living and the rhema gives direction in specific areas of their lives. The fruit of the Holy Spirit is their characteristic motivation, and the gifts of the Spirit are their manifestation to meet the needs of mankind. They are allowing their lives to become a prophetic expression of Gal. 2:20— "I am crucified with Christ; nevertheless I live; yet not I, but Christ liveth in me: and the life which I now live in the flesh, I live by the faith of the Son of God, who loved me and gave Himself for me."

PROPHETIC EVANGELISM

Evangelism is in the heart of God. Christ died to save sinners. Jesus came to seek and to save those who are lost. Evangelism was restored in the Evangelical Movement and has taken on new dimensions with each additional move of God. The Prophetic Movement is likewise adding a new dimension to evangelism. Saints are being instructed and activated in the supernatural gifts of the Holy Spirit. They are being trained within the church but the goal is to send prophetic evangelism teams into the highways and byways compelling the people to come into the Kingdom of God with supernatural spiritual ministry. The last move of God will be a "Saints" movement which will cause more souls to be saved than have been saved since the Church began.

Books on Prophets
Prophetic Movement & Ministry
by
Dr. Bill Hamon

"Prophets and Personal Prophecy" It is the biblical manual on prophets and prophetic ministry. Many scriptural proofs plus exciting biblical and life experiences revealing the proper guidelines for receiving, understanding and fulfilling God's personal words to individuals, churches and nations. More then 100,000 in print in eight different languages. 218 pages. $13.99

"Prophets and the Prophetic Movement" A complete overview of the Prophetic Movement, it's purpose and place in Church history in fulfilling God's ultimate destiny for His Church. Only in this book do you find the all important Seven Principles for determining a true restorational move of God.

Standards are given for discerning the differences between supernatural manifestations of Church prophets and people involved in the New Age, occult and other groups which manifest the supernatural. 227 pages $13.99

"Prophets Pitfalls and Principles" It reveals the pitfalls of weed seed attitudes, character flaws, and prophets syndromes found in the lives of several biblical prophets. The 10 M's for maintaining and maturing one's life and ministry are listed and explained. Answers are given to nineteen of the most common and complicated questions asked about prophets and personal prophecy. 224 pages. $13.99

Fulfilling Your Personal Prophecy

Pastors, make sure all of your leadership and members have their own copy of this vital booklet.

Everyone who thinks they have received a personal word from God needs this booklet.

Buy in quantity and give one to each person who receives a Personal Prophecy through your ministry.

SPECIAL VOLUME DISCOUNTS		
Number of Copies	**Price Per Copy**	**Approximate % Discount**
1	$3.95	
2 to 10	$2.96	25% Discount
11 to 99	$2.40	40% Discount

IF YOU BUY A FULL CASE OF FULFILLING YOUR PERSOANL PROPHECY YOU MAY RECEIVE A 60% DISCOUNT.

CHRISTIAN INTERNATIONAL SEMINARS AND MINISTRIES

SCHOOL OF THE HOLY SPIRIT

Local church Friday night meetings providing a place for prophetic ministry to the congregation and personally to individuals.

CHRISTIAN INTERNATIONAL MINISTRIES NETWORK (CIMN)

Teaching, training, and maturing prophets, prophetic ministers, a prophetic people, Apostles, and Apostolic churches.

CHRISTIAN INTERNATIONAL BUSINESS NETWORK (CIBN)

Teaching and activating Christian business people to succeed with biblical principles and prophetic perceptions, fulfilling their destiny.

CONFERENCE AND SEMINARS

Experiencing, establishing and activating into Prophetic and Apostolic Ministry

CHRISTIAN INTERNATIONAL PUBLISHERS (CIP)

Books, tapes, video's, and teaching manuals on prophetic ministry and restoration truths of the Church.

CHRISTIAN INTERNATIONAL NETWORK OF CHURCHES (CINC)

International Association of Prophetic/Apostolic ministers and churches providing training and accountability based on relationship.

MINISTRY TRAINING COLLEGE (MTC)

First semester anointed biblical teaching and the second semester mentoring and training in prophetic ministry and other areas.

MANUAL FOR MINISTERING SPIRITUAL GIFTS

A 300 page manual with two 2-hour video's - 13 weekly sessions - 26 activations - Certification required. For pastors and leaders.

CHRISTIAN INTERNATIONAL
BUSINESS NETWORK

Vision For Your Success

· ·

The vision of Christian International Business Network (**CIBN**) is to equip Christian business people to operate in the supernatural power of God and to practice biblical principles in the market place. In the day-to-day pressures of the business world, fortunes are made and lost based upon making the right decision at the right time. **CIBN** teaches, trains, activates, and mentors Christian business leaders in how to apply biblical decision making principles in this complex and stress-filled environment. **CIBN** also assists Christian business people in understanding their personal calling, and identifying their talents and gifts. Further, **CIBN** operates as a resource and networking center, bringing together Christian business people of like-vision and purpose in order to see the Kingdom of God established in the earth today.

CIBN offers opportunities for training and assistance in business through its newsletter (Christian Business Today), training seminars, local chapters, and consulting services.

Give us a call if you are interested in any of these resources at 850-231-2600 Ext 609 or write

Christian International
Business Network

PO Box 9000, Santa Rosa Beach, Florida 32459
Fax: 850-231-1485 or www.CIMN.net

KNOW YOUR GOD AND YOURSELF

MTC

FULFILL YOUR DESTINY

Our Vision

Christian International **MINISTRY TRAINING COLLEGE'S** vision is to teach and equip students in a practical and experiential way for ministry. Our approach to teaching and learning is based on the Elijah - Elisha principle: the impartation of knowledge, experience and anointing through a mentor-student type relationship.

Receive

* A one or two year on-campus Ministry Training College Education, Degree Program.

* Powerful classroom teaching in vital areas like Prophetic Ministry, Leadership, Practical Theology, Pastoral Counseling, Worship, Apostolic miracles etc.

* Practical and supervised ministry training tracks with major personal emphasis with balance between acedemic and practical preparation for ministry!

FOR MORE INFORMATION CALL 850-231- 2683 OR 850-231-2682 OR WRITE CHRISTIAN INTERNATIONAL, MTC P.O. BOX 9000 SANTA ROSA BEACH, FL 32459

VISIT OUR WEB SITE: **WWW.CIMN.NET/CI**

MANUAL

for

Ministering Spiritual Gifts

&

Student Workbook

"The Manual For Ministering Spiritual Gifts advances saints out of the realm of theory and brings them into a living experiential reality of God's graces. It is a manual designed for doing the Word, not just hearing it. This Manual helps teach, train, mature, and develop saints in their gifts of the Spirit while helping leadership to prepare qualified saints for use in various facets of team ministry."

by

Dr. Bill Hamon,
President & Founder of CI

Pastor, this manual will benefit your church and you...

* It will activate the gifts and ministries of the saints by providing 13 weekly sessions along with 16 corresponding spiritual exercises.

* It will stir and motivate your people towards spiritual ministry and their individual stewardship responsibilities of God's graces.

* It will build confidence and boldness in your saints by giving them opportunity to minister one to another.

* It will develop and mature your people in spiritual ministry without producing "spiritual spooks."

* It will deepen and strengthen your people's relationship with God as they are taught and challenged to hear His voice.

* It will furnish opportunity for church members to receive college credit for spiritual training through CI's School of Theology.

The *Manual for Ministering Spiritual Gifts* is available to those pastors who have become certified trainers. For information concerning certification for use of the *Manual for Ministering Spiritual Gifts* please call or write to:

CHRISTIAN INTERNATIONAL MINISTRIES NETWORK
P. O. Box 9000, Santa Rosa Beach, FL 32459-9000
(850) 231-2600 ext. 650

APOSTLES AND PROPHETS

THE COMING MOVES OF GOD

by Dr. Bill Hamon

• •

Foreword by **Dr. Peter Wagner**
Endorsements by **Oral Roberts** and many others

When apostles were active in the first generation Church, a great harvest of souls was brought in. When the apostles are fully restored, there will be the greatest harvest of souls ever. The whole world will be affected when the apostles and prophets are fully restored. Their ministries will signal the rise and fall of many nations and people. The restoration of apostles will activate the final three moves of God.

> The following topics are some of the chapters in Apostles - Prophets.
>
> Biblical perspectives of the ministry of Apostles
>
> Apostles and church doctrine
>
> Calling vs Commissioning of Apostles and Prophets
>
> God's desire and purpose for establishing His Church
>
> The special ministries of Apostles and Prophets
>
> The calling and ministries of fivefold ministries
>
> Divine progressive preparation for the Apostolic Movement
>
> Apostolic Movement and its potential extremes
>
> Last days ministries of Apostles and Prophets
>
> The Final moves of God
>
> The Saints Movement
>
> Army of the Lord and eternal judgment
>
> The Kingdom Establishing Movement

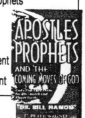

By the time you have finished this study on God's end-time apostles and prophets, a cry will start arising within your heart for the Holy Spirit to escalate His restorational process of God's holy apostles and prophets.

The Coming Saints' Movement

• • • •

What's next for the Church? Essential insights concerning the next restorational move of God. A must for those who want to be a part of God's last moves. Revelation of God's purpose for the Saints' Movement and what it will accomplish in the Church and the world. **$10.00** (Two 90 minute tapes)

Principles to Live By

• • • •

Bishop Bill Hamon presents six major Biblical principles that have helped him fulfill 50 years of successful Christian living and 47 years of ministry. **$30.00** (Six 90 minute tapes)

Plugging Into Your Spiritual Gifts

• • • • • •

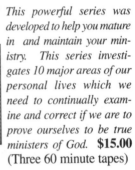

Dr. Bill Hamon's Tape Sets

T
h
e

10 M's

This powerful series was developed to help you mature in and maintain your ministry. This series investigates 10 major areas of our personal lives which we need to continually examine and correct if we are to prove ourselves to be true ministers of God. **$15.00** (Three 60 minute tapes)

Prophetic Pitfalls

This exciting tape series is an in-depth look at the pitfalls that face today's Christians. Dr. Hamon uses biblical characters to disclose the subtle satanic pitfalls which can cause leadership and saints to fall. **$35.00** (Seven 60 minute tapes)

CI's finest ministers in an array of teaching on the gifts of the Holy Spirit. This tape series will bring encouragement and build up your faith to manifest the gifts God has placed within you. **$30.00** (Six 60 minute tapes)

The Restoration and the Destination of the Church

A heavenly satellite overall view of the Church from its origination to its ultimate destination. The greatest information available on the progressive restoration of the Church unto its end time ministry and eternal destiny. The history and future of the Church from a Prophets view.

$50.00 (Ten 90 minute tapes)

•   •   •   •   •   •   •   •   •   •   •   •   •

Jane Hamon's Books

Dreams and Visions

Jane Hamon gives us an understanding of the seemingly hidden messages of our dreams and visions. It's time we learn to discern the voice of the Lord as He communicates His mind, heart, purpose and plan to us through the language of dreams and visions. This is the most biblical and balanced presentation ever written by a proven Christian Prophetess. **$10.00**

The Deborah Company

God is releasing keys of revelation and spiritual principles that will unlock the latent potential of power on the Church and bring strategic breakthrough in these important days. Women will have a unique part to play in this last days army that God is assembling. The time is at hand in which God is activating the gifts which have been deposited by His Spirit into every blood-bought, Spirit-filled believer, regardless of gender. It is a day for women to step out from under their cloaks of inactivity and step into their God-ordained identities as active, vibrant members of the Body of Christ. **$10.00**

ORDER CI PROPHETIC MATERIALS TODAY

BOOKS BY DR. BILL HAMON

Apostles, Prophets and the Coming Moves of God	13.99
Prophets and Personal Prophecy	13.99
Prophets and The Prophetic Movement	13.99
Prophets Pitfalls and Principles	13.99
The Eternal Church	13.99

Teaching manuals and workbooks are also available.

Prophetic Destiny and the Apostolic Reformation	6.95
Fulfilling Your Personal Prophecies	3.95

BOOKS BY EVELYN HAMON AND OTHER AUTHORS

The Spiritual Seasons of Life (Evelyn Hamon)	3.95
'NEW' God's Tests are Positive (Evelyn Hamon)	3.95
Redefining the Role of Women in the Church (Dr. Jim Davis)	7.95
Mentoring and Fathering (Steve Schultz)	9.50
Dreams and Visions (Jane Hamon)	10.00
The Deborah Company (Jane Hamon)	10.00

AUDIO TEACHING TAPE SERIES

Prophetic Pitfalls (Dr. Bill Hamon)	35.00
The 10 M's (Dr. Bill Hamon)	15.00
Plugging Into Your Spiritual Gifts (Dr. Bill Hamon and others)	30.00
The Coming Saints Movement (Dr. Bill Hamon)	10.00
Restoration and Destination of the Church (Dr. Bill Hamon)	50.00
Principles to Live By (Dr. Bill Hamon)	30.00
Handling Life's Realities (Evelyn Hamon)	20.00
Dealing With Life's Challenges (Evelyn Hamon)	20.00

PROPHETIC PRAISES CASSETTE TAPES AND CD'S

Show Your Power by Dean Mitchum (cassette)	10.95
Show Your Power by Dean Mitchum (CD)	14.95
Here's My Heart by Dean Mitchum (cassette)	10.95
Fan the Flame by Robert Gay (cassette)	10.95
Fan the Flame by Robert Gay (CD)	14.95

OTHER MATERIALS   Manual for Ministering Spiritual Gifts

Many more audio, video, cassettes, CD's and books available by other prophetic and apostolic ministers.

To order call: **1-888-419-2432**

Have your MasterCard, VISA or AMEX ready when you call!

or visit our website: **www.cimn.net**

CHRISTIAN INTERNATIONAL RESOURCES

P. O. Box 9000, Santa Rosa Beach, FL 32459

Prices are subject to change without notice.

Shipping Cost will be added to your order